How to Go from a Relationship
That Just SURVIVES
to a Marriage That Thrives

TALIA WAGNER, LMFT
ALLEN WAGNER, LMFT

MARRIAGE AND FAMILY THERAPISTS

LOS ANGELES, CA

MARRIED ROOMMATES

© 2019 Talia Wagner and Allen Wagner.

This publication contains the opinions and ideas of its authors. It is intended to provide helpful and informative material on the subjects addressed within. It is sold with the understanding that the author and publisher are not engaged in rendering medical, health, psychological, or any other kind of personal professional services in the book. All information is intended for general knowledge and is not a substitute for mental health advice or treatment. Always seek the help of your health care provider before adopting any of the suggestions in this book or drawing inferences from it.

The anecdotes in this book are illustrative examples derived from the authors' work. They are not based on specific events or people. Any resemblance to actual events or locales or persons, living or dead, is entirely coincidental.

print ISBN: 978-1-7335286-0-3
ebook ISBN: 978-1-7335286-1-0

Book cover design by David Provolo
Interior design and production by Domini Dragoone

www.marriedroommates.com

Newman Miller House
Los Angeles, California
info@newmanmiller.com

CONTENTS

INTRODUCTION

To this day, it isn't clear which one of us actually said it. Yet, once the word *roommates* was uttered aloud, it was like a bomb exploded in our living room. It was too late to take it back. Now it was out there and couldn't be ignored.

Regardless of who first called it, the truth was inescapable. After six years of marriage and two kids, we were in fact roommates. It was tough to accept that our amazing connection had dwindled into a stale transactional relationship of sorts, managing kids, house, careers, without much left over for each other. It was puzzling really—we still loved each other but were trapped in endless tit for tats and circular disagreements that went nowhere, just serving to fuel the mutual blame and mounting resentments.

Being marriage and family therapists, we did what came naturally—we talked it out to the point of exhaustion. The wheels started turning when we began to break down how we got to roommate status in the first place. Looking at our habits and routines gave us a clearer picture of how our relationship had gone adrift. Surprisingly, it also led us to see the same telltale signs of roommates everywhere we looked. It was a shocker to realize that most of the married people around us felt as if they were just roommates, too, be it our friends or our clients.

While this revelation made us feel marginally better that we weren't in relationship limbo alone, we started wondering what was going on in married households that led so many once happy and connected couples into becoming mere roommates.

We set off to find out.

Although it took us a long time to put all the pieces together and connect the dots, investing the time to research and understand this phenomenon probably ended up saving our marriage and those of countless clients along the way. Once we started seeing these same occurrences in relationship after relationship, we realized that a bigger issue was at play, and we saw its patterns everywhere. It was the same lack of fulfillment, frustration, and resentment, not just with our clients, but with everyone we talked to, which meant we were *all* doing it wrong—we simply didn't know how to be married.

The realization that we, like most, were grossly underprepared for life at this next level was a breakthrough. It wasn't anyone's fault. Nobody prepared us for what marriage and kids would demand of us, for how hard it was going to get, and for how we would need to adapt to meet these changes. Nobody explained that the rules would change on us, that we would have to evolve or else. The old playbook from our independent single lives had to be ripped up, and a new, more developmentally appropriate plan had to take its place. Easier said than done. Our initial failure to adapt to the changing circumstances exacted a high cost that we paid for with the well-being of our marriage.

Through our own experience, we know that being roommates is a lonely and unsatisfying place for couples. It is a state of emotional disconnect, where the fibers of connectivity and feelings of togetherness have slowly eroded. The connection and synergy that pulled you together in the first place got lost in the shuffle of life.

Stolen kisses, inside jokes, and pet names forgotten as you shoulder your shared load. No longer laughing and fooling around, finding each other's eyes in a crowd, or driving across town just to be together for ten minutes. It escapes your mind that you would have done anything for just a smile, that you used to make each other better by just being around. That you found inspiration and joy in one another, hearts pattering, dopamine levels peaking. There was heat and lust, interest and yearning—it was the fire, the energy behind your connection—all lost on the lonely road to roommates.

Married Roommates live parallel lives together. They subsist side by side, harmoniously or contentiously, performing their roles and carrying out routines. They handle their responsibilities and go through the motions of managing a shared life together, yet they do so with a critical piece missing. When the chemistry, lightness, and magic of being together disappears, there is an evident lack of emotional and physical connection. It is the reality for many couples who sit silently on opposite sides of the couch or sleep back-to-back, both feeling that an invisible wall separates them. These couples just exist together.

Most people have either experienced or witnessed this relationship state firsthand. These types of marriages are so common that some people simply believe that this roommate dynamic is what marriage really is, or what it will inevitably become.

The term *Married Roommates* describes couples who have reached the point where the only connection between them consists of family and household responsibilities, rather than the romantic or emotional connection they originally signed up for.

Many relationships end up in this unhappy and unfulfilling place. *Too many.* Time and time again, we have seen how subtle patterns of behavior toward one another evolve to become a "new normal" through which couples can easily drift into this disconnected and joyless state of Married Roommates.

THROUGH THE LENS OF COUPLES COUNSELORS

Being marriage therapists, we are entrusted with couples' personal stories. We hear what usually happens behind those proverbial closed doors—those secrets that people don't share with the outside world. Having seen thousands of couples between us, and having our own relationship as a backdrop, we have a unique understanding of what couples deal with and experience every day. The manifestation of Married Roommates is the number one reason that couples seek us out. The sheer number of couples struggling with this reality is staggering. Seeing the easy fluidity with which married couples can enter this state—the same issues playing out in home after home—has led us to realize just how susceptible long-term partners are to becoming roommates.

Resting on the assumption and illusion that your marriage can withstand a lack of intimacy and disconnect, it is all too easy to neglect the relationship and take one another for granted. It is so easy that couples actually don't have to do anything to get there. The disconnect happens automatically once you stop doing things for and with one another. Without putting in the work to maintain your marriage, this state becomes the norm, rather than the exception.

Marriages end up here and continue to deteriorate because couples allow it to. You do so passively, by not taking action or using ineffective efforts and poor tactics. Perhaps you are even unaware of the deterioration of your marriage, and, if so, your relationship will continue to wither until someone has had enough and slams on the brakes.

Many couples will seek help too late. By that time, their issues are so entrenched that it's that much harder to fix. Couples who find themselves living as roommates are often lonely, frustrated, and lost on how to move forward and regain the amazing connection they once had. For that reason, you must be proactive. You will need to work together to resolve your issues. Investing time and resources into your marriage now will inevitably save you from giving up *much* more time and resources later in a divorce.

A unifying name or label for this marital phenomenon has eluded public discourse—a necessary openness and conversation to truly examine and correct this predictable marital pitfall that turns our relationship into a platonic business of sorts.

Without an overall understanding of this paradigm shift, there was also no formal way or tools to tackle the stagnation and entrenched routines, other than therapy. Since not everyone has the interest or means to go to therapy, it was important for us to provide this information to anyone who wanted it, not just those couples we see in our private practice. By making our approach accessible, we hope to help as many couples as possible create a pathway out of the Married Roommate–zone and help them rediscover their relationship and partner along the way.

In writing *Married Roommates*, we aim to first expose and then eradicate the roommate phenomenon. We want to reach couples who are or may be at risk of becoming Married Roommates. Those could be the already married, the cohabitating, or even those still in the dating world, wondering how to think about and prepare for marriage. We want to give those couples and families hope that this is not just fixable, but also preventable.

In this book, couples will learn preventive rather than reactive strategies to improve communication, practice conflict resolution, and gain a more positive perspective of their partner. These methods and tools will inoculate your relationship from slipping into (or back to) roommate territory. With foresight, couples can thus be better prepared to protect their marriage from ending up in this very preventable place.

Married Roommates will equip you with the roadmap to get out of roommate territory. The book is designed to convey information in three distinct parts: The first will target faulty beliefs and irrational perspectives about marriage, which will help you change the rampant oversimplifications and misinterpretations that may be undermining your relationship. The second part offers tools to improve and correct communication, shows you how to conduct conflict resolution, and suggests tips for better connection, intimacy, and sex. These chapters will provide you with a new understanding of working as a team and teach you the strategies to implement a move forward through necessary reframes and new approaches. The third part helps you put it all together and create the paradigm shift that introduces a new normal where both partners work together toward building optimism, hope, respect, and a foundation of love and intimacy.

In fact, you and your partner can begin experiencing a better relationship sooner than you think. Progress just requires two people pulling in the same direction, toward shared goals. This is definitely achievable. All you need is a game plan with the right perspective, motivation, and the tools necessary to implement change.

We will show you the way.

PART I

MARRIAGE: THE MISSING OWNER'S MANUAL

All the universe labored

to bring us together.

The rest is up to us.

—BEAU TAPLIN, AUTHOR

MARRIAGE ADRIFT

Dreams of the Road Ahead

Josh was elated. He finally asked her, and she said yes. It took months to plan the perfect proposal, to get her family in on it, and to buy her the ring she wanted. His heart was still racing, but as he looked over at Tammi, it swelled with love and pride. After five years of dating, they were finally getting married.

Hours later, lying in bed together, Tammi's eyes still sparkled as she excitedly laid out plans for the wedding. They didn't sleep much that night, talking for hours about their future.

FROM TOGETHER TO MARRIAGE

Joining two lives in marriage is exciting. You spend hours dreaming of a future together, entangled in your visions and hopes for lifelong happiness. Couples excitedly whisper sweet promises to one another, envisioning deeply fulfilling years ahead. You fantasize about adorable kids who inherit her eyes and his smile and project your hopes into this imagined life.

At the onset of life together, you are eager and willing to put aside your differences. Sure, you may argue and disagree at times, but getting along is more easily achievable, as you want to forgive each other, rush to accept your own faults and mistakes, and happily engage in makeup sex. You spend your time thinking of how to make one another smile, splurging on the relationship, and prioritizing one another.

When thinking about marriage, you optimistically embrace the idea that everything will just work out. Your tastes and interests will gel together, and everything will fall into place. Your love will be enough to get you through all possible issues that may arise, and the spontaneity, intent, and fun will only get better from here on out.

While you have been warned by family members and friends that marriage will not be easy, it does not take much effort to dismiss that idea. You wholly believe that your expectations will become reality.

When the time comes for making the preparations for the wedding, you throw yourselves into the production—spending an enormous amount of time on getting everything for your big day to be perfect. There is usually so much to do that couples' attention and primary focus generally revolves around the logistics of getting married.

Down the road, you realize that the unfamiliar and challenging landscape of married life does not always fit the ideas and hopes that you had going in.

JOSH & TAMMI

Five Years Later

As the day came to a close and Josh still didn't say anything, Tammi realized that he forgot. It was their fifth wedding anniversary, and there was no gift, no card, and no acknowledgment. She was crestfallen. Josh had always made a big deal of celebrations, so his forgetfulness about this day was particularly hurtful. She thought back to his elaborate proposal, which involved all her family and seemingly half their town. He used to always be so over the top, but time had changed him.

Tammi glanced over at Josh sprawled on the sofa and couldn't help but feel sad. They had so many dreams, ones that she now knew would never happen. In those fantasies, he was going to open a restaurant and she was to be the head chef. That never happened. These days he still worked for his uncle, and she had to go back to work part-time at the preschool after their son was born. Money was always tight. There were months where it was so bad that she had to ask her parents for help.

Life didn't mirror their expectations, and they blamed it on each other.

THE REALITY OF MARRIAGE

Going into marriage, you theoretically understand that your life will change, but the awareness and insight of the reality of married life does not kick in until you are deep in it. As in Josh and Tammi's situation, expectations and beliefs are subjected to a metamorphosis when the day-to-day demands alter and real life settles in after the high of the nuptials.

Time fully crystalizes these changes, and only then does your perspective start to align with reality. The distance between our early expectations and real life can be massive, leading to letdown and disillusionment with your partner. Because you have unrealistic ideals going in, reality can disappoint and lead you to see what is actually normal as dysfunctional and broken. It is all too easy to feel duped and to see your partner as now different from the person you married.

A FUNCTIONAL AND EMOTIONAL PARTNERSHIP

The day-to-day reality of marriage forms a functional partnership, which joins the existing emotional one. The emotional bond is fueled by the love, fun, excitement, and sexuality between two people, while the functional one is the logical, realistic mechanics behind it. On top of making one another feel loved and connected, marriage means that couples now have to contend with big-ticket items such as career realities, financial pressures, health management, and retirement planning, as well as the more mundane functions like utility payments and food shopping.

The functional partnership starts a process in which you become increasingly dependent on one another for the ongoing maintenance of life. While it is initially exciting to build your home life and new routines around one another, as you settle in, time and regularity eventually transform the novel into the routine norm. The reality of creating a budget, taking out the trash, or dealing with a leaky roof are considerably less exciting and sexy. Although the functional side of the marriage must be managed or else, the emotional side often gets waylaid by the "busy-ness" of life. It is seen more as a luxury, "if there is time," which then upsets the balance of the two—the emotional and the functional—needed for a happy marriage.

Through the ups and downs of years of marriage, the priority between your roles as functional and emotional partners may morph in unintentional ways. The functional part tends to increase and mushroom in many different ways as you grow together, adding more appendages and spinning plates to your everyday life.

The dictionary defines *functional* as "intended to be used, practical rather than attractive"—an interesting definition considering that for many Married Roommates the functional begins to overtake the emotional and, with time, may be the only part of the partnership that survives.

Simple acts such as speaking to one another while multitasking robs you of the ability to be present with each other. So does eating in front of the TV, letting phones interrupt your time together, and going to sleep at different times. We see this process play out with our clients all the time—of course, priorities just naturally shift with time, responsibilities get prioritized over fun, work becomes more important than spending time together, efficiency overtakes quality, and we compartmentalize the good and zero in on the bad.

THE SHARED LIFE

During your marriage, you will create most of the long-standing systems of your life. As your family grows and your careers gain traction, life's demands require more of your time, attention, and focus.

What starts out as a small mom-and-pop operation with fewer duties and responsibilities grows in scale through the years. Couples must figure out how to juggle multiple balls in the air when it comes to their shared life. Shared life includes everything that couples jointly oversee and manage: the house, bills, schedule and planning, kids, extended families, social networks, chores, finances, employment, meal planning, and much more. It does not take long to realize that to manage this ever-growing list of shares success-fully necessitates a well-oiled machine of structure and routine.

These increasing demands can take you from being a young, carefree, and fun-loving couple to a busy, rushed duo, where responsibilities usually get prioritized over time together. You try your best to juggle the important events in life, but often your mar-riage gets lost in the shuffle—and many times is overlooked.

THE BUSINESS OF BEING TOGETHER

As the demands of domestic life pile sky high, couples' conver-sations typically turn into a long to-do list: *don't forget to pay the mortgage, call the plumber about that leaking pipe in the yard, write an absence letter for the kids, sign them up for that enrichment class, talk to the neighbor about moving the trash cans, and remember to call Aunt Sally for her birthday.* The list seems endless.

This reality of marriage usually leads couples to do an admira-ble job of maintaining the functional part of the relationship, but the intimate, emotional connection commonly stalls out. You get so busy taking care of building and upholding the infrastructure of your life that you often don't do as good a job of taking care of each other or, for that matter, even yourself.

In the beginning of the relationship, feeding your connection was effortless. Fueled by the excitement of a shared attraction, new couples naturally work hard to understand one another, to be supportive and complementary. Those behaviors reinforced your interest in one another and nourished the connection. However, that sense of newness—the butterflies and the desire to spend every waking moment together—does not last for most people over time.

TOM & CYNTHIA

Angry Silences and Loneliness

Everyone had gone home for the day, yet Tom lingered at the office. Nothing to rush home to, he thought. Life at home had changed drastically since he and Cynthia had gotten married last year. It started out great. They spent their honeymoon in Costa Rica, taking long walks by the ocean and making love every chance they got. They were inseparable the first few months after the wedding, but over the past few months something changed at home, making it increasingly difficult to stay positive and hopeful.

It seemed as if in the span of a year and a half, the novelty of marriage wore off. In the evenings they often found themselves doing separate activities, in different rooms. It felt as if they were drifting apart in other ways despite his attempts to figure out what else had changed. Cynthia resisted talking about it with him. Whenever he tried to discuss the state of their marriage, she insisted everything was fine.

Thinking about the last couple of months felt painful. He thought he knew what was wrong but had no idea how to fix it—especially with Cynthia's unwillingness to acknowledge the shift. Work had ramped up and he had multiple projects going at the same time, which sometimes helped because it kept him busy and distracted. This distraction would replace the constant worry he would cycle into, that she had fallen out of love with him or, worse, that there was someone else. Unfortunately, when he wasn't focused on work, he brooded on the issue.

As he gathered his things to leave the office, Tom dreaded the arrival home and the lackluster reception he would undoubtedly get from his wife. Tom couldn't help feeling that she didn't like him much anymore. Instead of fighting, she just shut down, freezing him out. There was no real way to tell what she thought, since she refused to open up. It felt as if he had tried to get through to her in so many ways, but it all fell flat. He didn't even try to initiate sex any longer, as he had grown wary of the constant rejection.

Cynthia heard Tom's key in the door. Not getting up, she reflected back to the days when she couldn't wait for him to get back home from work, greeting him at the door before he could even get his key out. She seemed to be doing a lot of reflecting lately. It made her sad. He came into the room and, without even so much as a greeting, continued on to the home office they shared. He would stay in the office for the rest of the night, except for when he came out to ask her about dinner.

As usual, they ate dinner quietly. Mostly he answered work emails at the table. It was normal. After dinner, he returned to work at his computer, then watched ESPN on the couch. Cynthia watched TV in the bedroom and eventually went to sleep around eleven. She used to try to get him to go to bed with her. She used to try to get his attention. She used to do a lot of things. Most of them she stopped doing and now only performed the most basic tasks of their life together.

He didn't say anything at first, probably didn't even notice, but once she rejected his flimsy attempts at finding a Band-Aid to repair their broken marriage, he was livid, and as payback, he started ignoring her. She didn't believe those attempts were real. Cynthia thought that Tom just missed having her waiting at his beck and call. She resisted talking to him, convinced that he couldn't change, so why even bother.

Few couples are able to maintain the initial intimacy of a relationship over the long haul. Not because it is impossible, but because once the newness fades, you stop putting in what you did in the beginning. As you grow used to one another, the urgency lessens and your behaviors predictably change to reflect this shift. Getting more comfortable with each other naturally reduces your efforts to impress, to make sure that time spent together is fun and exciting. You may call or text less, dress down more, and those romantic evenings out on the town happen less often, if at all. You may give each other the perfunctory kiss in the morning and evening, but you get too busy to think about calling one another during the day, just to say hi or share a funny story that happened on the way to work.

As a result, couples who start out with incredible attraction can end up flatlining. Those who once couldn't take their hands off each other, or found it hard to be apart, now rarely brush up against one another or even think to send a text throughout the day.

Conversations have become mostly a means of information sharing, instead of lively dialogue and interested chatter. Interactions that would have formerly been flirty and fun have become no-nonsense to-do lists and "don't forget" reminders. Any sort of romantic connection and passion between two people gets absorbed into the mechanics of daily living. Interactions are devoid of connecting moments, and the everyday operations of living together become the essence of the relationship.

That's how you become Married Roommates.

Worlds Apart

"I'm leaving!" Janna called out as she closed the front door behind her. Most evenings, once she tended to the kids' homework and evening routine, she usually went back to the office for an hour or two to plow through all the paperwork on her desk. It was better than sitting next to Gabe on the couch just watching the evening shows.

She wondered when precisely their relationship had downgraded to this uninspiring tedium. Other than living in the same house, it felt as if she and Gabe shared nothing in common. They hadn't spent time together or showed interest in one another in a long time. Gabe wasn't a bad man. He worked, took care of his responsibilities, and loved his kids, but it felt as if they were worlds apart.

Does this sound familiar? If it does, and you feel that your marriage is going down this path—taking you from passionate lovers to mere roommates—this book may serve as a wake-up call. It's time to prioritize your marriage over other activities that have taken over as you drifted away from one another. While that task may seem daunting, your marriage is more than repairable, if you put the work in. And we're here to help.

At the end of each chapter, we will bullet point the main ideas and thoughts.

Let's get started.

CHAPTER 1

KEY TAKEAWAYS

✔ The reality of marriage does not always meet the expectations, hopes, and dreams that you had going into it.

✔ Many times, we are blinded by the fantasies in our head. We are so excited about our joint future that it is hard to see that we are romanticizing marriage and our partner.

✔ Joining two lives together is hard, because we largely go into it unprepared, and we don't create two separate lanes for the functional and emotional. This allows the responsibilities and duties to overpower and rob us of the fun, light, intimate moments of our connection.

✔ These increasing demands can take you from being a young, carefree, and fun-loving couple to a busy, rushed one, where responsibilities usually get prioritized over time together.

✔ The emotional connection dwindles because we stop putting in what we naturally did at the onset of the relationship. We allow our energy, intent, and time together to be taken over by the functional—conversations become about logistics, responsibilities, and duties, which muscles out our connection.

✔ Few couples are able to maintain the initial intimacy of a relationship over the long haul, not because it is impossible, but because they don't try as hard as they did at the beginning.

✔ Practicing prevention through maintenance will go a long way toward preserving the emotional bond and create a protected lane for a couple's intimacy that is now being rerouted into the functional stressors of life.

LIFE'S THREE ACTS

Newlywed Bliss

It was a few months out from Ray and Mackenzie's fairytale wedding, a destination wedding in Mexico that, although few of their family and friends could afford to attend, was incredibly romantic and picturesque. The high of the perfect getaway wedding wore off quickly once they got home and their new reality quickly had them both on edge.

Ray and Mackenzie moved in together after the wedding, preferring to keep their individual apartments while they were dating. It worked for them then, but it certainly wasn't working for them now. Although they both agreed that Ray's apartment was preferable in size and convenience, sharing the space was proving to be far less comfortable than they imagined. Mackenzie was realizing that despite what he said, Ray was territorial about his stuff and didn't want her to make any changes. Ray was learning that letting Mackenzie move in meant that every item he owned was now being considered as worthy or not. He got

progressively more upset as he found himself defending his
furniture, kitchen appliances, and closet space.

He lashed out at her a few times when he came home and
found she had reorganized and thrown out a bunch of his music
memorabilia. This had been happening with alarming regularity,
and at some point, he finally had enough and unfortunately drew a
boundary that ended up hurting her feelings and causing a huge fight.

Mackenzie didn't understand his problem. She was making
tremendous efforts to build them a home. So what if she wanted
to get rid of some of his rag-tag crap? Him fighting her about
every towel and spoon she wanted to chuck was proving to be
a tedious uphill battle. She was starting to suspect that he was
a bit of a hoarder. Every time she tried to throw anything out, he
would rush in and start going on and on about the sentimental
value of the most ridiculous items.

ROMANTICIZING MARRIAGE

When it comes down to some of the more predictable challenges of marriage, society does not do its part to prepare us for the road to come. As a culture we tend to romanticize the wedding process, glossing over the often-unmarketable realities of marriage.

Young couples focus their attention around the excitement of the wedding, the honeymoon, and everything that lies in between. The dress, the guest list, the invites—the to-do list leading up to the big day is an exciting blur. Fixated on the details of putting together this exciting moment, you usually don't talk about what happens *after* the honeymoon, when life gets real and you must figure out how to braid two individual outlooks and mindsets into a harmonious adult life. Young couples getting married for the first time usually don't think about the challenges of maintaining their love and connection through the years among all the twists and turns that life brings. This lack of insight leaves many going into this major life change ill-equipped and underprepared for the difficulties ahead. As a result, many will have a hard time adjusting.

The truth is that getting married, unbeknownst to them, propels a couple into Act II of their lives.

The Acts of Life is a phrase that has been used in many contexts. From a developmental perspective, psychologists have loosely referred to it in explaining different stages of human development. We utilize this phrase as a reference point to specific developmental markers of an adult life. Breaking down the three acts helps simplify the abstract and complicated topic of normal adult development. We use this framework in our practice to assist clients with gaining the awareness and insight needed to achieve success in life. This assists them to understand that one's outlook and input must evolve to meet these markers or there will be real-life consequences to contend with.

These three acts are loose expectations of where one should be at any given point in life, based on healthy development stages that adhere to societal norms. Your twenty-year-old self should be quite different from your forty-year-old self in the way you act and behave, in your goals and lifestyle, but will these changes just occur naturally? Do you just organically evolve and mature to meet these unspoken expectations of life, or must you actually take steps to facilitate this growth?

Will the forty-five-year-old dad accept and understand that his insistence on being a "night owl" is now costing him and his family his much-needed strength, clarity, and patience? When he wakes up late and strolls into the kitchen grumpy, is he able to connect the dots to his wife's subsequent "nagging" and disapproving looks, or does he just find a way to rationalize his behavior to himself? What about the wife who, along with her husband, owns a profitable business and loves their comfortable lifestyle but refuses to learn anything about finances and money management because it's "too hard"? And how about the guy who refuses to give up buying parts for his toys (such as cars), although it means struggling financially? Or the mom who will not entertain changing her style of dressing sexily, despite it being an embarrassment to her kids and husband?

Let's look at the evolution of the stages of life in context.

THE FIRST ACT

Act I sees you through early adulthood, moving from being a dependent to self-reliance and independence. This era is characterized by important personal achievements, experimentation, and uncertainty. For many, it is a time of complete self-absorption and self-discovery, during which you learn to become more comfortable in your own skin.

Act I generally gives you the space and freedom to develop your individuality. Living on your own, college, first jobs that morph into careers, and coupling up in mature relationships characterize the act's major milestones. During this time, the focus is on yourself, and, in accordance, your reality and behavior are shaped through the lens of yourself as a *self-driven, individual entity*.

There are opportunities and options available to you during each act that are unique to that time. They may be available but not necessarily appropriate at later stages. Maybe your dream was to be a traveling musician or study Spanish abroad, and while it is never too late to make such wishes a reality, if you missed the opportunity in Act I, you may have to wait a long time, until the responsibilities of Act II fade out, for those dreams to become a reality again. Some opportunities may be lost to you forever, such as sowing your wild oats before marriage, and you may just have to accept that you missed that boat and do so without lingering resentments.

Often the transition from one act to the next is not seamless or short; it can take time and induce significant growing pains to realize and accept that life can't or won't stay the same.

THE DUO OF ACT II

Act II officially kicks off when you commit to a life of "we" instead of "me." Pairing up, you chose to go through life's adventure alongside a partner, and, whether married or not, in Act II you share your life with another. This can be a tough transition, where you are all of a sudden expected to go from making choices for and by yourself to now having to compromise, find middle ground, and share all elements of your life with one another.

A perfect storm of troubles can be created where, in a condensed period of time, couples build a family, a home, the infrastructure of their lives, and their career—*all at once*. While these are theoretically wonderfully amazing milestones, the level of obligation and selflessness required comes as a shocking surprise for most.

ELLIE & IAN

Co-juggling Reality

Ellie was anxious for Ian to get home. Since they began renovations on their house, her days were filled with a parade of subcontractors. She had a newborn baby vying for her attention, as well as her two older energetic kids who were home on spring break.

She had not stopped going since dawn, and her head was splitting from a never-ending barrage of tasks coming from all sides. Between the kids, her own job, and the house responsibilities, she was hanging on by a thread.

When Ian finally walked in thirty minutes late, she met him at the door, passed the baby to him, and went into their bedroom, slamming the en suite bathroom door in anger. Ellie hoped the shower would calm the waves of resentment she felt toward Ian for being late once again. She felt that he left the hard stuff to her, using his demanding job as an excuse for the lack of engagement at home. He felt he was doing his part with his salary and financial support. So the demands of family life rested at her feet, and he didn't even seem to care.

After all the talks and discussions, he still didn't get it. This was not going to fix itself, but he refused to read the marriage self-help books and articles that she suggested. And every time she brought up therapy, he got indignant. Ian absolutely refused to entertain the thought of talking to a stranger about their struggles, insisting they could fix their issues on their own.

■

Ian had a rough day at work. His boss had chewed him out in front of the whole team for being late. The morning routine with the kids always got him out of the house later than he wanted; Ellie never understood how much traffic he had to battle every day into the city because she worked from home. As usual, his late start meant he needed to stay late to make up the time. Again. Rush-hour traffic home stressed him even more. He tried to make business calls in the car and would often work at home in the evenings to get ahead of his workload, but it was not enough. It barely made a dent in what had become his new normal—a much higher than expected output at work and at home.

Typical Ellie, throwing the baby at him as soon as he walked in the door. He needed a break himself, but there seemed to be no way to win. He often didn't know what more she wanted from him. Between home and work, he was busy every second of the day, yet Ellie seemed to think he had spare time. The moment she would catch him doing "nothing," she would extrapolate it into a general behavioral pattern as opposed to an occasional stolen moment—if that—he managed to get for himself. Between his bosses at work and his wife at home, he felt constantly criticized. The constant ribbing from Ellie robbed him of what had been his typical upbeat nature prior to getting married and having kids.

Once Ellie was out of the shower, she helped Ian get the kids ready for bed. Since she always insisted on reading to the girls, most nights she just fell asleep with them. It used to bother Ian that the only real time they spent alone as a couple were the few moments in the mornings, to steal a quickie before getting the kids up and ready. Now, he just felt tired and didn't want to argue, so he just once again passed out on the couch watching TV.

Couples are often not prepared for the stressors and difficulties that accompany life's major accomplishments in Act II. Getting married, having kids, having more kids, moving to a bigger house, and advancing in their career—all ultimately create greater expectations and more responsibilities that you do not have the infrastructure to support, since you are still operating with the insight and habits from Act I, which now come up significantly short.

NO WORRIES, IT'S "NORMAL"

The additional spinning plates that you both balance as you advance deeper into marriage and family is normal and actually predictable if you really stop and think about it. The reason you often fail to manage these increased demands in life and in your relationship has more to do with your inability to anticipate and change expectations and/or behaviors accordingly than your inability to do so. It is as if the treadmill you were running on just sped up, and failing to adjust your speed accordingly, you fall. If you knew that the pace was about to change, you would have been ready for it. The insight that in Act II every part of your life will change and that this is "normal" eludes us.

You often don't think about or prepare for the compounding effect of growth. Perhaps your career trajectory changes, making the forty-hour workweek morph into more like sixty hours. A bigger family has more needs, leading expenses to naturally increase. Perhaps you make the leap from renting and buy a house, perhaps a house that needs work (because when don't they?). Repairs, landscaping, malfunctions, breakdowns—all have now become *your* problem. Expenses that you did not have to account for in Act I now abound, and you must learn new skills or expensively outsource these new demands.

The same challenges occur with your time, as scheduling for more people and events naturally requires logistical maneuvering worthy of a drill sergeant. More preparing, planning, and budgeting requires an increase in input from both of you, which inevitably gobbles up even more time and energy. And the cycle continues.

Every moment now seems to have multiple demands placed on it, but instead of working as a team, you split the load. You end up going at it alone, which just makes it harder. By doing so, you eliminate more and more of what you need to support one another to meet these increased demands. You spend less time together, and less time alone or with friends. You stop doing what makes you happy, eliminating hobbies and other avenues of self-care, now seen as luxuries. You cancel the monthly get-together with friends at the basketball courts or golf range. There is no more yoga, playing pool, or lunches at your favorite restaurants. But by eliminating these, you cut out much of the fun and joy of life.

RAQUEL & BRAD

Overwhelmed in Unison

Raquel sat in the pouring rain watching her son, Evan, play soccer. Other moms huddled around, jabbering about some celebrity gossip. She pretended she was on a phone call to avoid joining in.

Evan ran by and waved, and she was able to muster a thumbs-up and pasted on a grin from ear to ear. She hoped it looked believable. She could imagine the amount of work calls and emails overloading her phone, which kept vibrating. She knew some of the vibrations were a group text planning a "girls' night." Another thing to do. It's not like she didn't like the women. Their kids were the same age, but they seemingly had all the time in the world to plan these elaborate nights. For her, the time and financial cost, as well as the burden of getting Brad to babysit, always led to conflict. She knew she should probably respond to the women soon or the phone calls would start and she couldn't handle that, not today. She still had to pick up her daughter, Megan, from a playdate.

The thought of more work emails coming in caused her head to throb. She was closing in on a promotion at work, and the company's biggest client had personally selected her to run point on the new project. She had tried to tell Brad about the magnitude of it, but of course he didn't seem to care. It was the increased work hours and her time away that he cared about.

Work on weekends and girls' night out were almost taken as an affront to his value. He didn't understand the sacrifice she made for their kids, like sitting in the pouring rain so Evan could see her smile and feel supported and proud. It was all part of the bigger picture, but somehow, he saw her as selfish and nonempathetic toward him.

Brad had called earlier to ask her to pay some bills he was "too busy" to deal with, because she was "doing nothing anyway." She had already knocked off the grocery run, prepackaged the kids' lunches, and put the last load in the dryer. Plus, dinner was defrosting. She tried to contain her rising resentment, not wanting Evan to read the disgust she felt toward Brad in that moment.

Brad's heart was beating erratically. He had been banking on the same raise he had gotten last year, in addition to the yearly bonus. But his boss just informed him that due to cutbacks, the bonuses were not happening this year. He struggled to think of a good way to tell Raquel. They planned around these events as a given and had already booked the summer vacation to Yellowstone.

In truth, it was Raquel who had really pushed for the trip, although he begrudgingly agreed, in part because she would take every opportunity to remind him that he had promised her this trip two years ago. He tried to talk her out of it, worried about the finances, but she convinced him that with his bonus to cover it, there was nothing to worry about.

"Fuck," he kicked the trash can under his desk in frustration. As if this shitty day wasn't enough, he couldn't just go home and relax, as he still had to be "on" for daddy duty. Brad was so angry, but he didn't bother calling Raquel to commiserate, because past knocks had shown him that she wouldn't care.

She texted before he left the office to tell him that she had paid the bills, which was a relief, but then she added even more errands to his day, asking him to swing by Home Depot to pick up toilet cleaner, and, oh, stop at an ATM for cash for the school pizza party. There was also her earlier text to swing by the grocery because she also forgot to pick up the cupcakes for Evan's class party. The more stops he made, the more his mood plummeted. Brad couldn't help it. He dejectedly thought of the kitchen sink full of dishes that would be waiting for him, and the homework and bedtime routines with the kids. It was like he never got to breathe.

A massive mental shift must happen for us to be ready for the demands of this act. Coming from a place of solely indulging your individual wants and needs to this advanced level of togetherness, teamwork, and partnership can be jarring. Not understanding these life transitions in advance, and what they will need from you, has couples walking in blindly and winging it, which makes it that much harder. Your day-to-day functioning may necessitate change, but instead of adjusting that mindset accordingly, you often fight it—sabotaging yourself by not fully comprehending that seismic changes must be made to your lifestyle, decision-making, and ability to work as a synchronized team in order to truly succeed together.

light of the realities and demands of Act II, it is almost inevitable for couples to drift from a place of understanding and having empathy for each other to a place where it is easy to find fault with one another's choices and decisions. Instead of upping your ability to lean on and support one another, you end up resenting and blaming each other, which leads to feelings of being taken for granted. By personalizing the hardship and not seeing that this shift is a normal part of life, it is easy to think that your marriage is failing—and to feel like a victim.

While your responsibilities at this stage of life certainly grow, you don't have to take an all-or-nothing approach. Unfortunately, you stop doing much of what you did to take care of one another before, and by doing so you unknowingly allow the distance to grow.

Because you are not prepared for these normal upticks of life, most couples feel exhausted and overwhelmed. You have nothing to give each other at the end of the day, preferring to just focus on your own needs instead of one another.

Married Roommates can rationalize their lack of time or energy toward each other as the natural ebb and flow of periodic relationship downgrades, as long-term relationships naturally have some stretches of time that are better than others. Through seeing these as normal ruts indicative of the ups and downs of marriage, couples diagnose their distance as a temporary problem. They falsely think that this state will eventually fix itself. But the danger lies when this pattern becomes the new normal.

People often leave it up to chance, ignoring the warning signs and avoiding the idea that the relationship may be in trouble. By doing so, they unknowingly move themselves toward a more permanent roommate dynamic.

Although this is a common reality in many long-term relationships, Married Roommates rarely disclose their marital deficiencies. Instead, they usually keep the internal workings of marriage between them. If they would share their challenges with friends or family, they would probably find that many of them are in the exact same predicament.

Our culture often paints a contradictory picture, where social media platforms provide daily posts and visuals of what look to be happy marriages, thriving kids, and successful lives. These bombard you hourly. Through this lens of viewing selective moments in the lives of friends and associates, most of us speculate, fill in the blanks, and assume. When you see images of others in love, holding hands, and enjoying each other's company, you may wonder why *your* marriage isn't as fulfilling. Even if you recognize these visuals as edited illusions that do not fully reflect reality, they can still affect you emotionally and lead you to create a false story of your own to mask what you see as lacking in your own life.

The general lack of openness in society does not allow us to normalize and adjust our expectations. You think that you are the only ones failing at managing it all. Embarrassed, you embellish happiness with friends and family, presenting a facade of holding it all together. There is a general sense of dishonesty about how hard Act II is and how much you struggle. There is no public discussion or acceptance of what is a very real and compounded stage of life. In its lacking, you feel as if you must pretend that everything is awesome. Because you believe that everybody else seems to be doing just fine, you emotionally beat yourself and your partner up in your mind and real life, not wanting to feel you are failing.

LENORE & JAMES

An Edited Reality

Lenore's phone buzzed for the fourth time. She knew it was the girls commenting on her best friend's photos from last night. It made her feel petty that she was so affected by those pictures of their anniversary dinner. She knew her reaction had nothing to do with her friend's actual relationship; it was more about her own envy and lack of fulfillment. Still it bothered her that it was never her who got wined and dined at the best restaurant in town. Her own anniversary came and went with little fanfare, as it did almost every year. Another friend got a huge bouquet of flowers delivered to her office last month and now this.

It often made Lenore feel like her husband was not as thoughtful or that maybe he didn't love her as much. She never shared those thoughts with the girls, feeling pressured to post visual evidence of her own happiness, validating to herself that she was living a life that was just as great. She was guilty of editing her online life to omit any signs of disconnect with James, not wanting anyone to see the cracks. Online, they appeared to be the best and happiest couple with an active social life. But this facade she put out there made her feel alone in an already lonely reality. She knew her friends wouldn't or couldn't understand, so she just kept it in.

THE MONKEY WRENCH OF TECHNOLOGY

Technology has changed just about every facet of human interaction—marriage being no exception. It has ushered in a whole new reality of life, and, as a result, modern marriages must contend with challenges not encountered by any previous generation. While innovation and ease has worked to better many avenues of daily life and experience, it has also left a negative mark on all of us. More than at any other time in history, people feel alone.

Nowadays, technology has superseded the importance of direct human contact in almost every part of our lives. It is easier to reach for our devices than it is to reach out to those we love.

Technology has made it easier to bury our heads in the sand, to be distracted and avoid what is happening at home. It can help to mask problems, allowing you to virtually avoid, ignore, and evade the fact that you are roommates and that it sucks. You get busy reading the news, playing games, perusing social media, and logging a play-by-play of your life while virtually (and literally) ignoring your spouse. You probably don't even feel bad that you haven't exchanged a word all evening—it now feels normal.

Modern day society has normalized pulling away from your real life to set up the ongoing selfie or to take time away from being present on date night to get the perfect picture of your sushi plate. Smartphones have shortened attention spans and really stunted people's ability to stay present and enjoy the moment.

This book is not the place to go on about the dangers or costs of crossing the line with regard to the use of technology, other than to note that these influences are real and can damage your relationships with others and your relationship with yourself. You are not always able to see that clearly, as the human mind can find a way to rationalize, justify, and explain away just about anything. You may not recognize that there is a problem until it has caused serious enough consequences for you to stop and take note. You can use preventive measures to place boundaries on the use of electronics, especially when it starts to become a substitute for moments in your real life. Take heed of this issue and protect yourself (for example, put the phone away in the evenings, or enforce no electronics at the dinner table).

THE REALITY OF BUFFERS

As the years pass, technology helps many roommates escape their reality. Children and responsibilities also become buffers by distracting from the emptiness and lost connection with one another. Contentment and joy come from your kids and family life, rather than from your partner. It creates a skewed family reality, where the scope of partners becomes child-centric, sending the wrong message to your children about love and family. Each partner martyrs themselves, forsaking their own happiness for the sake of the children.

Your marriage matters a great deal to your children. They benefit directly and indirectly from seeing you happy and content with one another. Children receive a lot of benefits and value from homes that have both parents, but what's even better for them is to come from homes where parents love one another and cherish their connection and time together.

Inevitably when the children grow up, leave, and take the happy energy with them, it is only then that many couples realize that through the years they grew so far apart that now they feel like intimate strangers. That realization is many times the end for some Married Roommates.

Empty Nesters

Ruth sighed deeply. She debated going downstairs to make some tea, but she gave in to her sadness and got back into bed. Getting the call from Eva canceling their lunch pushed her more deeply into this funk. She knew her life was transitioning now that her youngest child was in college. Her home life with Larry had changed dramatically in the past few years as their kids grew and needed them far less.

Becoming empty nesters hit them hard. They hadn't adjusted well to all the free time they now had. They had been so involved with their kids that they hardly noticed their barely existing connection. Ruth hadn't known how much their rift had cost them until the kids left, leaving Ruth and Larry alone in a big, empty house with a shell of a marriage.

ACT III: A TIME OF OPTIMISM OR HOPELESSNESS

Act III can play out like those *Choose Your Own Adventure* books where, depending on the choices you make, you get one of two endings. This can be a time of great happiness for a couple or a time of deep sorrow as realizations may lead to separation and divorce. Interestingly, the more recent statistics on divorce have been decreasing for most age groups except one. If you guessed that those impacted are mostly empty nesters, you are right. The statistics indicate that gray divorce is on the rise.

Ideally, if couples are able to hold onto each other through the hardships of an earlier and more challenging time with mutual respect, communication, and love, Act III is where you enjoy and reap the rewards. Life slows down, with fewer responsibilities and fewer balls to juggle. The kids are now grown—most likely at college or off living their adult lives. Their demands on your life are minimal. Employment should be ramping down, leading toward a time of reduced workload and/or retirement. That means more time on your hands doing what you love.

If you did it right, this could be the best time of your life. If you cherished your relationship and nourished it through the years, it will be there intact in Act III. Together you will get to enjoy the fruits of your labor. You get to enjoy your grown children without having to discipline. Perhaps there are even grandchildren down the road. You get to appreciate the time you have together and the money that you will have hopefully saved, and go on to build your dreams together. Otherwise, the statistics on gray divorce are not hopeful.

You may decide that pulling your life apart is too hard and settle for a life lived side by side. People are capable of building happy, independent lives from each other. They are also capable of remaining miserable side by side, sad, and lonely. So, much of what happens here depends on which adventure you choose. The flipside is that you go for the gray divorce, opting to take advantage of the years left and really live them on your own terms.

GETTING TO THE FIX

Regardless of the act of life you may be in, it is not too late to correct course. Whatever neglect, resentment, and stagnation has taken root in your marriage is fixable. It takes learning to communicate with one another in a way that actually works, and there is a way, believe us—it's a two-pronged approach of removing the bad and rebuilding the good. Many couples come to therapy when their home life becomes intolerable. They work on removing the bad, and the environment at home improves. Some erroneously believe that this lack of bad is good enough and do not continue the work to rebuild the good, which robs them of the potential for soaring to new heights in their marriage. We encourage couples to use the two-pronged approach to avoid settling for the good-enough marriage.

In the next chapter we will explore marriage's need for a team mentality. We look at why it is so critical for couples to become a unified front and warn about the breakdowns that may occur when they don't function as teammates.

CHAPTER 2

KEY TAKEAWAYS

✔ Society often glosses over the unmarketable elements of marriage—choosing to focus on its shinier and more romantic aspects. This romanticizing of marriage works against young couples, who inevitably spend their time and resources now on efforts that will not serve them down the road.

✔ This lack of insight leaves many going into this major life change ill-equipped and underprepared for the difficulties ahead. As a result, many will have a hard time adjusting.

✔ Couples are often not aware of the intricacies involved in this higher level of adulthood. It is then easy to blame it on each other, to have resentments toward who has it easier, and to get caught up in the problems, rather than look at the solutions.

✔ Act II means living a shared life, where you now must function as a duo. This requires you to work together to make decisions and choices that propel you forward.

✔ There must be a massive mental shift for partners to have the abilities and tools to make it through this time of life, intact as a team. Just getting married, without having this awareness, can easily set you up for failure.

✔ You can prepare for predictable changes. And you may have to accept aspects of your life that no longer fit into this act.

✔ It is easy to personalize the hardships of Act II and blame each other. Society may reflect back to you that you are the only ones struggling, that this is not the reality in many homes and in that it becomes your personal problem, rather than a systemic one.

✔ Technology can mask the problems of your marriage, working along with your bad habits to keep you away from one another, in avoidance and mindless exhaustion.

✔ Couples get stuck and assume that a lot of this behavior is normal and that the distance they feel from each other is temporary.

✔ The years could pass, filled with buffers and distractions, but one day, those will dwindle and come to a stop, and you will be forced to face each other and the relationship you have created.

✔ It is never too late. Even those in Act III can find their way back to each other.

✔ You do not have to settle for the good-enough marriage. Use the two-pronged approach to fixing your connection—learn to work to remove the bad and rebuild the good.

WHERE DID WE GO WRONG?

Loners and Lovers

Hal had a rare morning off. He planned to leisurely sip his coffee and just relax on the couch. Mia flew into the kitchen, ready to attack the day with her usual go-getter attitude and high energy. His wife was quite the personality and he loved her for it, but sometimes she exhausted him with her insane multitasking.

When he got home last night, she was busy making modifications to her e-commerce site while engaging in a group chat with friends and watching her weekly tv show. He tried to get her attention, but as usual, she was juggling a million tasks and he just let it go. They both worked really hard as parents, had a beautiful home, and were truly appreciative of the roles they both played, but he felt disconnected. For Mia, life played out in order of priority, and between the kids, her extremely successful business, their home, friends, and social life, their relationship never seemed to crack the top three. He knew she loved him, but sometimes it felt like she didn't know him, because if she did, she would know how much he missed the girl he first fell in love with. It saddened him that she couldn't see the importance of prioritizing their relationship.

Mia hated it when Hal started in on their lack of time together. He knew how busy she was, and acting like she was prioritizing everyone else over him was not fair. She didn't know how to make him understand that the business and kids just needed her more, while he was fine to manage himself. It felt overly dramatic to her to say that they had no time together; it was just the reality of being busy working parents. He needed to just get over it.

While it may not satisfy the romantics among you, marriage functions much like a business—the business of being together and successfully managing your shared life. Those who are entrepreneurs or own their own business inherently understand the importance of working *on* your business, in addition to working *in* it.

Take, for example, a plumber. Yes, he has to do the actual work of fixing a leaky faucet or a broken toilet. But the work doesn't end there. He has to work at maintaining and building a client base, continuously advertising his services, keeping tabs on finances, and accounting for what money comes in and out, as well as managing staff. Marriage should have the same level of investment. Working on your relationship creates accountability and growth in ways that just going through the motions daily will not.

THE IMPORTANCE OF WORKING ON YOUR MARRIAGE

Going into marriage, you often don't realize how absolutely necessary it is to manually maintain the quality and longevity of the relationship. You do not fully understand that the emotional bond between you needs constant work to continue to thrive. From that perspective, many of us do not know how to be married.

Most of the couples we speak to seem to have a general lack of awareness that the relationship as an entity needs ongoing work. It simply does not occur to them that the marriage itself requires maintenance. They see the relationship as a function of what it serves in their life as co-parents, financial partners, and so on. They give little time or effort to thinking about their union of a couple as its own entity. This is where the marriage is neglected, until something goes wrong. That is when many people spring into action, newly determined to save their marriage.

It's this reactive approach that we discourage; instead, we encourage couples to go for a more preventive approach, where the ongoing commitment and investment from both parties safeguards and protects the relationship from the breakdowns, fights, and disconnect that would otherwise plague it.

This limited perspective of marriage isn't your fault. At the onset of marriage, you weren't given a pamphlet to guide you through maintaining a good and healthy marriage. No one truly explained or walked you through the difficulties and frustrations you will inevitably face together, especially when you may have markedly different ideas about your home, family, or money.

Having this skewed outlook on marriage leads many to erroneously believe their bond to be strong enough to withstand the ups and downs of life without ongoing maintenance. Unfortunately, that is a falsehood. Your connection is like a living being that needs to be nourished or it will wither away. This bond must be fed and protected; otherwise, you will become, at best, roommates who still have regard for one another, in a friend-like or sibling-like manner. At its worst, the relationship morphs into ugliness and contempt.

MELANIE & MANNY

Is This All There Is?

Melanie felt lonely. She had been married to Manny for two years, and as much as she tried to avoid thinking about it, she knew something was missing. The idea of marriage had seemed so much more exciting and optimistic in her daydreams, but in reality it was a far cry from such fantasies.

Melanie wanted more out of their relationship than the static routine they had settled into. They hardly ever fought, and for the most part acted respectfully toward one another. They shared the household chores, enjoyed hanging out, and had nice, supportive friends that they saw regularly, but there was no excitement or passion anymore. They were best friends playing house. The unspoken monotony of their days weighed heavily on Melanie. There used to be small gestures, special glances, or intimate touches between them, but that never happened anymore. Their sex life was equally monotonous—a quick grope or two and it was over within a few minutes. It was just mechanical and most of the time felt obligatory.

She tried to talk to him about these feelings, but he would just get mad. From Manny's perspective, they had a great life together. They had a nice house and good cars, and they had the time and money to do whatever they wanted. He saw it as naive and unrealistic that she wanted more out of their relationship. He thought she was trying to change him into the guys from the romance novels she was so fond of. Manny thought she was being ridiculous and didn't want to talk about it anymore. His silence left Melanie feeling hopeless.

Manny didn't understand his wife's obsession with love and being in love. He thought he understood marriage, in ways she didn't. She expected romance, rainbows, and butterflies, but that wasn't realistic. While Manny was used to her emotional overreactions, he just hoped that her discontent would pass soon. He didn't know how to engage and remind her that they had a great life together. He too was at a loss.

THE BEST AND WORST OF ROOMMATES

At their best, Married Roommates can have the greatest of friendships. It is a relationship between two people who genuinely respect and love eachother. They live together harmoniously, supporting one another, and enjoy spending time together. Those in this category have a great relationship, but it feels much like a platonic one. There is no sexual chemistry, attraction, and fiery interest in one another.

While being married to your best friend is a giant pro for most marriages, as roommates, even the best of roommates may find that they miss out on having sexual intimacy and experiencing passion. These are integral, nonnegotiable parts of a romantic relationship, and when it is missing, it impacts the emotional connection, making the marriage feel incomplete.

These roommates may share a high degree of nonsexual intimacy, like snuggling on the couch, supporting tough times at work, or being on the front line of family drama. They may seemingly be content with this situation, as this type of intimacy has its strengths. Nonetheless, it is not enough to sustain them as individuals or as a couple over the long haul of life together.

When the romantic side of the relationship gets suppressed by the other roles you each play—co-parents, business partners, roommates—the connection once shared feels lackluster. While some couples may find themselves content together despite being roommates, most are not.

On the other side of the Married Roommate spectrum are couples who are disconnected from each other. They live largely parallel lives under the same roof, functioning together but emotionally alone. They may become withdrawn or passionately angry, as they lack the friendship and intimacy that the Married Roommates have in the previous scenario. Instead, there is a deep divide. These couples negotiate the logistics of their lives and share the load either politely but disaffected or with anger and resentment piled into every exchange.

Most couples find themselves somewhere in the middle of the spectrum—that gray zone between being best friends and disconnected frenemies. Regardless of whether things at home are politely calm or easily escalated, being Married Roommates feels crappy. The dynamic of your exchanges is laced with an edge. There is an unfulfilling routine-ness to your life together, a distance and emptiness that feels like a vast void. As resentment builds on both sides, you stop working as a team, and the connection continues to suffer for it. Once that occurs, the relationship feels like it has fully shifted into roommate territory.

TONY & RACHEL

Alone Together

Dinner was finished. Tony put away the dishes and wiped the counters, while Rachel read bedtime stories to the kids and got them ready for bed. When she came back downstairs, Tony was busy on his phone, and she took that as an opportunity to scroll through her Facebook feed. They didn't talk to each other as they both used the downtime to de-escalate from the long day and mountain of responsibilities they shared. Ten to fifteen minutes later, when they were sure the children were sleeping, they settled in to watch their weekly shows. They didn't talk much after that, either. When Rachel got up and went to bed, Tony didn't follow her upstairs; he stayed put watching the late news. Their nights were always the same. The routine varied slightly from day to day, but all in all, this had become their new normal.

More so than in any other part of life, Act II needs the dreams, hopes, and fantasies that we had in Act I. You need it to believe in each other, to believe that you are in it together, and that you have each other's back. You need it to stay positive and motivated to keep going and enjoy this stage of life. But for Married Roommates, that doesn't happen. Let's take a closer look at what you can do to turn that stale dynamic around.

BUILDING COLLABORATION AND ALLIANCE

You have the power to change your reality, but it must start from a place of teamwork and collaboration.

Imagine two partners attaching themselves to an invisible potato sack. From that point forward, they must hop along together, in unison, in their shared life, managing to move forward with all the subsequent ups and downs that life brings them. Moving together as a unit, potato-sacking it up the mountain ahead, is hard. You must continue your hopping—together—through the good, bad, and ugly. There will be plentiful and lean times, but the only way you will get up that hill is to work together.

While this is a predictable stage of life, many were not taught that the journey will undoubtedly get harder. When it inevitably *does* get harder, some couples find it difficult to adjust. They would do better if they were able to foresee that life's challenges would require better tools to continue to get along. Developing effective communication and conflict resolution skills can only assist them to make it through intact as a couple.

SAMANTHA & JERRY

Individual vs. Team Vote

Samantha was swamped at work. For weeks she had asked Jerry to plan their Fourth of July weekend away. While he hadn't booked anything yet, he had a couple of ideas that he hoped she would like. His work was also ramping up, and the trip just seemed to keep sliding down his to-do list, getting bumped for things that had to take precedence. Every time she asked him if he had made headway with the trip, he could feel her disappointment. Jerry knew she took this personally, as the goal of the trip was to work on their relationship and reconnect again.

They didn't get to take time away frequently, so when Samantha dropped the bomb that she had talked to her brother and asked him and his girlfriend to join them on their trip, Jerry was speechless. While he knew how close she was to her family, this was supposed to be their romantic weekend away. It didn't make sense to him. Was she being purposely vindictive because he took too long to book it?

His mind cycled around all the times that he was a team player when it came to her family. Anytime that he resisted going along with these shared family activities, Samantha would accuse him of disliking her family. It was a frequent and old fight that he thought marriage would change.

He was apprehensive about confronting her with his feelings. Whenever this topic was brought up in the past, Jerry felt dismissed. He didn't understand why she could not see his perspective. They were married. She was his wife, dammit. Why couldn't they do things together without other members of the family? It was crazy that she was not able to cut the cord from her family.

Samantha watched the conflicting emotions play out on Jerry's face. She knew he wasn't a fan of the big family outings and shared activities that had always defined her family, but she thought he would come around after they got married. Jerry's family was so small and distant. They never spent any meaningful time together, and they definitely never took vacations together. It was the complete opposite of her family.

Samantha couldn't understand why he wouldn't take joy in the fact that they could all be together on this vacation—the more, the merrier. She knew that he felt she disregarded their plans, but that *was silly—they could still have a romantic and special time, even with her brother there. She was sure that he would get past this resistance. She was convinced that all it would take was time to get him to be a part of the family.*

FLYING SOLO VS. JOINT SOARING

Making decisions unilaterally generally fails. So does forfeiting your vote by allowing the other to make the decision alone. Doing so allows you to blame and point fingers when the result is not one you agree with. Being adults and managing a shared life is hard enough, but doing so as a fractured unit makes it twice as hard. Samantha should have asked Jerry first, before making a unilateral decision about their vacation. Being a unit means that decisions like that should be made together. Doing so circumvents the anger, resentment, and hurt feelings that would otherwise surface.

It is important to go into this union with the understanding and acceptance that marriage represents a trade-off. You give up some elements of individuality for the stability, reliance, and growth that you gain as lifelong allies. You get a partner for life's biggest adventure, a cheerleader, and a built-in support system to worry and care for you. There's someone to help you fight life's dragons and create a safe haven from adversity. Not to mention, you get the privilege of having another to commiserate with, bounce solutions off, and learn from.

Once you can see it as so, you can move forward in attempts to find a balance, a compromise where both partners are agreeable and release the idea of blaming your spouse for begrudgingly giving up some of the things you used to do and be when you were on your own.

> **WE SAY:**
>
> Don't underestimate the simple idea of picking your battles. Oversights and mistakes will happen, but not all will be of the same magnitude. Be choosy in how you react to these. Build in an extra step prior to reacting of checking in with yourself to see if it is worth going to battle for. We encourage our clients to practice letting go of the unimportant. Next time the credit card bill is paid late, or the car is on empty, practice letting it go by asking yourself if this act is important enough to lose an evening of your life over. It may feel extreme to ask yourself if it is worth your marriage and your connection, but ultimately that is what is at stake.

A NECESSARY SHIFT

While marriage does not include a roadmap, it does determine that we will go through life's obstacle course as a duo, a unit. Whether that unit is successful or unsuccessful depends on the couple's recognition that they are now a team and their ability to learn to act as teammates.

Society's focus on individuality creates a "me and mine" approach that does not align with the mindset needed to see your union as a collective. An "every man for himself" mentality works against your marriage. This idea that we can still maintain the individual mindset with regard to tasks, money, family, and decisions is something we witness in couples' dynamics on an almost daily basis. This undermines their ability to be a united team and works against a successful marriage.

Despite this reality, many couples insist on holding on to their individual paths, keeping their resources separate, whether that is their bank accounts or social networks. They work in opposing ways rather than working together to create joint systems and strategies. Couples may fail to realize that the insistence on individual self-gratification and self-interest creates a mine-versus-our perspective that leads to each person focusing on getting their own needs met first and foremost.

Today's trend of getting married later doesn't help the situation. Each person coming to marriage later in life means that while they may be more emotionally mature, they are also used to being self-reliant and independent for most of their adult life. Having your personal well-being as a primary focus for so long creates deeply ingrained habits and behaviors. Making the mental shift and the adjustment necessary to be a working team of two does not happen automatically. The idea of sharing a life, where self-sacrifice, reliance, and dependency are a necessity, does not just come together on its own volition.

Teamwork must be developed and maintained. It will not just gel together without ongoing input from its members. Acting in a manner outside of our own self-interest and desires does not always come naturally, even if it is our intention to do so. It's a learned behavior.

When the perspective becomes one of a *team*, you see that working together toward a common goal allows you both to win. A united front helps a couple to develop an open-minded approach to discussing problems without defensiveness, anger, or blame. Failing to do so creates an uncompromising black-and-white, all-or-nothing perspective. There is a winner but also a loser. In that way marriage can feel like a seesaw, transitioning between one party at the top, while the other grazes the bottom. In the marital seesaw, the goal is to equalize by meeting in the middle, for compromise is the only way to reach consensus.

JONAS & REED

Pet Peeves and Provocations

The doorbell rang, and Reed's eyes almost popped out of his head when he saw their friend Matt outside with groceries. He really disliked it when people dropped by unannounced, but he hid his annoyance and gave his guest a friendly greeting.

He took the bags from Matt and went into the kitchen, hurriedly trying to clean up the cluttered countertops. As he was grabbing Matt a drink, his phone beeped with a text from Jonas, giving him a heads-up that he was stuck in traffic and that he had invited Matt to dinner. Reed's annoyance flared right back up. This was so typical of Jonas. Reed was very clear that for him unannounced houseguests were a no-no. Being a perfectionist, it was important to him that his home was clean and organized when they had guests over. Jonas knew this, so his text felt like a diss to Reed. He responded with an angry text, and then tried to compartmentalize his anger so that Matt wouldn't pick up on it, which would only serve to make him uncomfortable.

It was only when Jonas got the text from Matt that he was running early that he realized he had forgotten to run the evening's plan by Reed. Shit. This would not go over well. Reed was the least spontaneous person he knew. It was ridiculous, but Jonas knew Reed would freak out, as he had many times in the past. The pissy text from him confirmed Reed's suspicions. It pissed Jonas off that Reed felt that he could dictate how his social life was going to be run. Jonas had always been a fly-by-the-seat-of-his-pants kind of person. He didn't usually make plans till the last minute, and that's the way he liked it. He didn't appreciate Reed's inability to compromise on this issue, and it angered him. He kept ruminating all the way home. It didn't end up being a good night for either of them.

IDIOSYNCRASIES AND IRRITATIONS

Letting pet peeves and growing annoyances take hold and spread from your thoughts to your behaviors will trap you in an endless cycle of unhappiness. Seeing the good or bad in your partner is a choice you ultimately have to make every day, and focusing on what they do wrong or what they don't have can spell disaster in a relationship.

Like everyone who walks on this planet, your mate will undoubtedly have faults, just like you do. No one is perfect, and everyone makes mistakes. At times they will make judgment errors, oversights, and bad decisions that may cost you both. It's hard to cut your partner some slack or to make one another feel loved and cared for when all you can think about is what they did wrong. Generally, their intention is not negative or destructive, although it may produce a poor outcome. Seeing these mistakes as ones made by bad intentions hurts you both.

Letting negative thoughts about your partner take hold in your mind poisons your marriage. Give one another the benefit of the doubt. You cannot be a good friend to someone you see as an enemy, and unfortunately that is where many formerly happy marriages end up.

Although your partner will at times let you down, disappointment is a two-way street. When your spouse does something that you don't agree with, it is important to talk yourself off the ledge by reminding yourself to let go of the inconsequential rather than dwelling on what may have happened and getting stuck in your negative feelings. Move away from cycling around the problem to moving forward toward solutions. Your goal should be to work together as a team to navigate minefields, mistakes, and distractions. Any approach other than an aligned partnership against the problem pits you against each other and spells trouble down the road.

SARA & DANNY

Where Did the Love Go?

Sara was feeling apprehensive ahead of her fortieth birthday. While she was busy from sunup to sundown with the kids and her internet business, she still felt unfulfilled, empty, and bored. Her life felt like an endless series of chores with nothing to break up the monotony. She tried to think of the last time she and Danny got a sitter and actually had fun with one another. Their relationship seemed to be held together by their kids and endless responsibilities. The only time he touched her anymore was when he gave her the perfunctory morning kiss goodbye.

She had a hard time understanding how they got here. They met in college and had a steamy romance for years. Always together, happy and connected. People used to envy the love they had for each other. They were the couple everyone bet on to last forever, and yet here they were. She remembered the elaborate birthdays he used to plan for her in the past and doubted if she would even get a card this year. She held in a lot of her anger and resentment, not wanting to go on fighting, as they did in the past. Although their home was quieter now that they didn't fight anymore, it also left them with little to say to each other. These days they were all business, conversations clustered around daily activities, the kids, family, and business. There was never any mention of their relationship or the sorry state of their intimacy. She never brought it up and neither did he.

Danny was watching Sara frown into the mirror. He knew that she was thinking about her upcoming birthday. He had been thinking about it as well. He could not get himself to plan anything for her. While he helped the kids buy her a few trinkets, he didn't want to plan anything elaborate. It was about time that she got a taste of her own medicine. She was always stressed and running around doing a million things for everyone else, except for him. Danny could not remember the last time she said something kind to him or about him. But she had no problem picking at his faults and shortcomings. He never did that to her, and it hurt that she saw him in such a negative light.

ACCEPTING DIFFERENCES AND ALIGNING EXPECTATIONS

The way we relate to one another, handle interactions, build expectations, and follow through is rarely thought out. Back-and-forth contact is usually a free-flowing dynamic, which is largely automatic. Without awareness and attempts to change, individual viewpoints will continue to hijack our ability to work together toward a shared goal.

If you want events to play out differently, you will need to negotiate to strike a balance and find a middle ground that is beneficial to both parties. Take into consideration that the core concept of marriage means that you don't get life on your own terms. You must give and take and make concessions for the greater good. This doesn't have to be you solely sacrificing. It is a constant balancing act between the partners' and the family's wants and needs.

Communication and compromise are so important that without them, that metaphoric potato sack keeping you together begins to rip apart at the seams. Learning to problem solve effectively moves you both toward compromise, where it is easier to understand and negotiate, rather than doing so from a place of distance, where each of you stands firm and unbending in your interpretations and beliefs.

Underlying differences in viewpoints, values, and beliefs must be communicated and then compromised on. You need to learn to recognize and accept your differences; trying to change them does not work. In order for your connection to remain positive, it is crucial to learn to accept one another and respect the fact that you are different.

HEATHER & GEOFF

Explanations and Excuses

Heather was fuming. It was the day of their daughter's softball game, and Geoff was nowhere to be found. She couldn't take her eyes off Natalie's dirty uniform. Today was supposed to be their family's turn to provide for snack day, which she had piecemealed with some probably expired granola bars and the last of their juice boxes. She was used to thinking on the fly and coming in with last-minute recoveries for Geoff's oversights, but not washing the uniform made her feel like all the other moms were looking down at her.

It was a sweltering summer August day and her shirt was already sticking to her back. She tried to not overthink the stained uniform and enjoy the game. She prayed that Geoff was running late because he was getting the portable shade tent that he ordered online and that she wouldn't have to brave the entire game under the sun's merciless rays.

Geoff ran from his car when he realized he was already more than ten minutes late to the game. The donut place had a longer line than he had expected, but he was excited to get the kids something sweet for snack time. Heather's disappointed or rather borderline maniacal face clued him in to her negative mood, as well as his taste in snacks, and he knew it was going to be a long two hours. When Geoff saw the Gatorade-stained shirt, he knew he really messed up. Work and some drama with his own family left him scattered. Some things just seemed to fall through the cracks. He was already sweating, and without sun coverage he and Heather were going to have a miserable time in the unrelenting heat. He had meant to order the tent on Amazon.

PROBLEM-SOLVING AS A TEAM

Getting to the top of career or academic achievements requires accountability to keep us organized. In school, if we don't perform, we fail. At work, poor performance can cost us promotions or, worse yet, the job altogether. In relationships, people rarely have this sort of accountability. They lack intention and thoughtfulness, which often works to their detriment.

The countless small steps that it takes to become Married Roommates are composed of endless individual choices, behaviors, and attitudes. Those seemingly insignificant moments serve to move you further away from your mate. If you can change those interactions to more positive experiences for both of you, the opposite will happen. Instead of moving away from one another, you will grow closer as a team.

REFLECTIONS ON DOING THE WORK

Some might balk or resist doing the work that they need to do to sustain a healthy relationship. They may refuse to utilize the reframes or strategies necessary to make the changes needed for improvement. They may have a negative attitude or give up when it starts to get more challenging. Those same people don't usually stop and consider the alternative. What happens when you don't do anything to fix it? Does your relationship stay static or do you deteriorate even further? What if it could actually not be as painful as you imagine, but make your life better?

From our experience, one partner usually sees any change in the system or additional expectations as more than they can handle. This partner usually resists finding solutions, which only leads them to risk their own happiness, sense of freedom, and hopefulness.

While it is true that it is a bit harder to do things differently when you are set in your ways, the path there usually does not take more time or effort than is already being expended. The solution is about redirecting that time and effort into habits that yield better results.

Going in, most couples don't realize that practicing prevention is the only way to stop the tide from pulling you under. Once you are battered and bruised, it is much harder to hold on to one another. See the effort that you put in today as an investment in your future happiness. If you do the hard work now of learning to function as a collaborative team, effectively communicating, resolving conflict, and maintaining the relationship itself, you may avoid the harder work you will have to do later.

FIXING ON YOUR OWN

Some partners may recognize the disconnect and push to fix the relationship before it is too late. They may find a willing or unwilling partner. Since a good or bad marriage is determined by the commitment from both partners, it can certainly complicate things when each partner wants different fixes.

In particular, it may be challenging to have your partner even see the disconnect. If that is the case, the one ringing the relationship alarm will get frustrated with the lack of interest or responsiveness from their partner, which makes it easy to get progressively angry or further detached and to pull away and shut down—which inevitably will just make the situation worse.

This stage is a common enough reality, and although it makes getting to the fix more challenging, change is possible. If this scenario sounds familiar, don't lose hope. You may need to address it a bit less directly, but it is repairable. This issue will be further addressed later in chapter 8.

In the next chapter, we will look at further reframes and strategies necessary to change the unproductive patterns that led you to become Married Roommates in the first place. We will focus on the challenges with communication that couples regularly face and examine positive and negative dialogue—words that help and harm.

In addition to the effective communication reframe, we will highlight specific tools that will change this dynamic to a more positive and constructive one. We break down and clarify the changes couples need to make in order to be more successful in understanding one another.

It is important to see these as a two-pronged process, both necessary for lasting change. The reframes in the coming chapters will assist couples to remove the bad, while the tools will help to rebuild the good.

CHAPTER 3

KEY TAKEAWAYS

✔ Your relationship needs ongoing work to survive.

✔ Marriages are often neglected until something goes wrong. This reactive approach must change to a preventive one, focused on maintenance and ongoing commitment and investment from its members.

✔ Your bond is not strong enough to withstand years together without fixes, course corrections, and a strong emotional bond. You will have downturns, but you must recover by pulling yourself out of stagnation, not just accepting it as normal.

✔ Roommates can be good or bad friends. Home may be calm and loving or contentious and combustible. What Married Roommates all lack, though, is the right romantic, emotional connection to be a couple.

✔ Change this reality by working together as teammates to tackle problems and at the same time to rebuild your emotional connection.

✔ Work together to make joint decisions—even on seemingly individual issues. You are now a team, and you will benefit if you learn to navigate life as a unit.

✔ Situations will play out differently if you negotiate and find common ground in compromise. More often this will get you to a win-win situation rather than a lose-lose.

- ✔ Underlying differences in viewpoints, values, and beliefs must be communicated and then compromised on. You need to learn to recognize and accept your differences because trying to change them does not work.

- ✔ Redirecting your time and current habits will take work, but the payoff will be enormous. On the flip side, failing to address issues that will continue to deteriorate without your involvement kicks the can down the road where the options to save your connection will be much more limited.

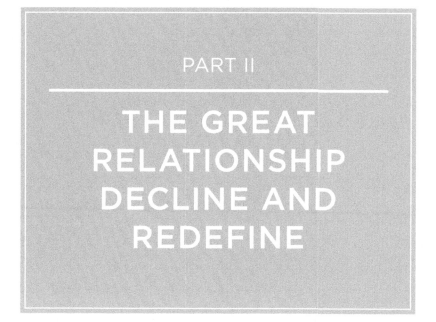

PART II

THE GREAT
RELATIONSHIP
DECLINE AND
REDEFINE

A great marriage isn't something that simply

happens; it's something that must be created.

—FAWN WEAVER, AUTHOR

4

COMMUNICATION CORRECTIONS

LAINEY & STEWART

Are We on the Same Page?

"Can you come outside and help me bring in the groceries?" Lainey asked, speaking into her phone as she turned onto their street.

"Okay," Stewart said, "I'll meet you outside in a minute."

When he came out, Stewart waved a quick hello, went to the trunk of her car, and reached for the bags. Suddenly he stopped, and in an instant, he was furious.

"Did you seriously go back to the outrageously expensive Farm Fresh, when just last week we specifically talked about cutting back?" he spat out accusingly.

Lainey's heart sank. "You act like I was out getting facials," she said. "This food is for us, not the neighbors. Not only are you not appreciative that I do all the shopping and cooking, but now you act like I'm the one sabotaging our family."

She was so angry she slammed the car door and walked toward the house.

"I was just trying to save us money by eating at home," she muttered on her way inside.

"Sure you were. Keep telling yourself that," Stewart shot back.

They didn't talk the rest of the evening or for most of the next day, choosing to stay away from each other.

NEGOTIATING THE SHARED LIFE

Communication is an area of the relationship that couples often find most difficult to negotiate. What makes these transmissions in marriage so tough as opposed to communication in other relationships is that marriage itself ties you together in a unique partnership. This bond creates an all-consuming personal, physical, emotional, and financial investment between two people—one not replicated in any other relationship.

The shared life requires two previously independent people to now share their possessions, time, abilities, and resources. Through this shared life couples must learn to navigate the blending of two often differing opinions, belief systems, values, expectations, and experiences into one combined life experience. This is obviously not an easy process to navigate, and, whether or not you are aware of it, the only tool you have to negotiate your differences and reach compromises is communication.

It's through true conversation that a couple can figure out and negotiate both functional and deeper emotional issues. Creating useful dialogue is critical for you to understand one another, especially as you set about establishing and managing your shared life.

Getting it right is crucial; there is no other way to reach the consensus necessary to build a meaningful life together.

WHY IS COMMUNICATION SO HARD?

People are incredibly complex. More so than any of us can fully grasp. The human brain is still an enigma—one that is highly intricate and perplexing. Since we are not neurologists, we're not going to inundate you with complicated scientific information on brain and human functioning. That said, it is important that you have a basic understanding of how the brain interprets stimuli in order to understand that the way you perceive your spouse's verbal and nonverbal behaviors does not always reflect reality. To begin, let's showcase an example in action.

CARLOS & SANDRA

Unintentional Letdown

It was the one-month anniversary of their quickie wedding. Everyone thought they were crazy to elope after two months of knowing each other, but Carlos and Sandra just knew they were meant to be. Carlos was excited to make this anniversary dinner for Sandra and show off his better-than-average culinary skills. For the past week he was busy planning the perfect evening. On the day of the date, a couple of Carlos's friends from college came into town unexpectedly. He was hoping to meet up with them after dinner and show off his new wife in the process. He texted her to see if she could get out of work earlier, feeling excited that she would finally get to meet his buddies.

Sandra read the text with growing unease. She didn't even have the time for dinner tonight, let alone time to hang out with his friends. It was simply not going to happen with the deadline she was up against. She sent back a text, letting him know that she was swamped, and that perhaps it would be for the best if he saw them tonight and they pushed the anniversary dinner to tomorrow. Sandra knew how much these guys meant to Carlos, and she thought he would jump at the chance to hang out with his boys. So she was surprised when she didn't hear back from him.

Carlos was crushed by Sandra's disinterest. He was shocked that Sandra would not prioritize this evening, which was a perfect opportunity to get to know his friends. She knew that they saw each other infrequently and how important it was to him that she meet his friends. Carlos did end up seeing his friends that night, but he wasn't really present. He was in his head, thinking that maybe they did rush to get married, seeing as Sandra's work and ambition seemed to be her first priority.

DECODING AND ENCODING IN COMMUNICATION

The encoding/decoding theory of communication was developed by Stuart Hall about media messages, but it is useful in understanding the communication breakdown between two people. Don't get scared off by the lingo; it is pretty simple to understand. With every single expression, either verbal or nonverbal, you send a message. All expression has meaning, yet each party assigns different interpretations to the same expression. In order for communication to be effective as a tool, both parties have to encode and decode the message correctly. Encoding is the process of producing the message, while decoding refers to the process of interpreting and understanding it. Any error between these two processes, whether in transmission or receipt, can lead to the information sent and interpreted in a completely different way.

Frequently the intention and the interpretation are not one and the same. In the example, both Carlos and Sandra had faulty interpretations of their back-and-forth communication. Sandra assumed that Carlos would prefer to spend the evening with his friends. She didn't communicate her rationalization with Carlos, nor did she explain the reason behind why she wanted a rain check. If Carlos had that information, perhaps he would not have personalized her response and taken it so hard. Carlos also didn't share with Sandra the reason he wanted her there; in its absence, it was easy for Sandra to assume and go with her faulty interpretation, as it was for him. It is unfortunate, as this misinterpretation led to a major misunderstanding and cooldown in their new relationship.

Although you probably believe that you respond directly to the happenings in your environment, internally the process is much more complicated. Your brain identifies external stimuli received through your senses and then interprets this data by turning what you saw or heard into meaning. This interpretation is what you actually respond to.

MAX & KATY

Perception vs. Reality

Max walked into his wife Katy's catering store with several packages in hand. As he rounded the corner, deep in thought, he looked up to see Katy and her new employee standing very close together in the back office. He did a quick double take, noticing their positioning and proximity in the storeroom—not to mention their startled reaction to finding him standing there. His eyes widened, screaming with unspoken suspicion.

Perhaps nothing happened here; perhaps something did and Max's reaction was warranted. The point is that your mind makes connections, attaches occurrences and moments, groups them together, and gives them meaning. Many factors contribute to why you think the way you do and interpret events so distinctly. In Max's case, his immediate suspicion had to do with his prior history of being cheated on. Max was hyperaware of men and sometimes went overboard with jealousy due to his prior experiences with unfaithful partners.

Behind the scenes, your senses are hard at work, sending in an enormous amount of material every second about your surroundings and interactions. Your brain works tirelessly to interpret these stimuli and make sense of them, using your background and experiences to do so. The wide variances in our personal stories make for vast differences in interpreting and making sense of our world. The most notable influences on our perspective are gender, culture, age, personality type, family of origin, and personal life experiences.

If a laid-back guy named Brian walked into the store and saw the same scene playing out with his wife, he might have noted it, then rationalized it as her being close and playful with her employees, ultimately, thinking nothing of it. A totally different reaction than Max's, but then again, Brian never experienced the betrayal of infidelity. His trust had never been broken by a significant other, so loyalty was not even something he questioned.

TRUTH IS SUBJECTIVE

Because your perceptions are subjective, your interpretations are formulated in ways that are specialized to you. What you were exposed to in early childhood and subsequent adulthood—the people, places, food, travel, even what you consumed in media—all leave their marks in various ways. These experiences help shape the way you see and interpret your world. Max became a less trusting, more suspicious person because someone violated his trust. That impacted him years down the line, in that moment in time with Katy, although he wasn't actively thinking of it.

These differences determine why one person can take an offhand utterance as an insult, while another takes it as a challenge, and yet someone else takes it as a joke. Conversely, it explains why one person will give you the chance to merge ahead of them on the freeway, while another will angrily speed up and cut you off, each one right in their own mind.

The takeaway here is that people do not think or process their world in the same way. That is too simplistic an idea and does not do justice to the incredible abilities of the human mind.

Unless you know someone's internal dialogue, you cannot always know or understand the complexities behind surface communication. All you know is what your mate or anyone else says or does, which is many times devoid of the underlying meaning or context. Not having this subtext is a major obstacle to effective communication, as faulty assumptions easily take over even the most benign interactions.

GOING DEEPER AND DEEPER

Failing to communicate appropriately has much to do with not going deep enough to explain the feelings and needs behind what you express. Without understanding each other's subcontext and intention, you and your mate operate in a vacuum, left to your own devices to read into clues and cues. This leaves the door wide open for misunderstandings, faulty interpretations, and assumptions, which can and will run rampant.

This situation can also be true when a partner has a history or precedent of a specific behavior, which is easily linked from the past to the present through misinterpretations.

AMBER & WYATT

Jumping to Past Conclusions

Wyatt had a long track record of flirting with women. Since his marriage to Amber two years prior, he frequently assured her that he was a reformed flirt and that his player days were behind him. Although his behavior used to be the trigger for many of their arguments, Amber thought they had long put that issue behind them. So when she came back from the bathroom at the restaurant and saw him smiling and nodding at the young hostess, she stood frozen in shock. Amber was so incensed that she grabbed her purse and walked out, leaving Wyatt to chase after her in surprise.

"What's wrong, babe?" he asked as he caught up to her in the parking lot.

Amber turned away from him. "I can't believe we are back to this. The minute I turn my head, you flirt with any halfway cute girl."

He looked at her in disbelief.

*"I was **not** flirting with her; I was just trying to get us a table!"*
he said. "Amber, we've been through this before. That part of my
life is over. I wouldn't hurt you like that again."

THE BRAIN'S ROLE

The human brain seeks to understand, to make sense of the world and your place in it. When missing a piece of the puzzle, it fills in the blanks with its own interpretations. You do this automatically. When Amber came out of the bathroom and saw her husband talking to a hostess, although she couldn't hear what he was saying, she didn't stop and think rationally about what she was witnessing but rather went straight to emotional despair. Wyatt's smiling at the waitress was a fact, but it was Amber who gave the moment meaning—interpreting it based on an old behavior. Your brain intuitively interprets situations and then gives them meaning, leaning heavily on subjective feelings, preconceptions, the past, and half-truths to get there.

Coming home to a quiet house, a husband looks around the kitchen and thinks, *She didn't cook tonight?* His interpretation: she must still be angry about yesterday. Thinking about it, he gets upset again. *I can't believe she's taking it this far when she was wrong in the first place.* His faulty interpretation continues to get fed by his negative perception.

In reality, his wife had a busy day. She did not get a chance to run to the grocery store and thought they would just eat out. When she got home and noticed her husband's short responses, she immediately attributed it to the night before, thinking he must want to continue the same dispute.

JULIA & SERGEI

Insufficient Impressions

When Julia saw the charge from Sergei's card on their joint account pop up on her email, she hung her head in defeat. She had never heard of "Brook's," but she figured it was just another expensive lunch. They had been through this countless times. She couldn't be his personal police, stopping him from spending. After numerous attempts, she finally got him on the phone and he was evasive, leading her to fear the worst—that he was lying again.

When she got home, he stood at the door behind a huge bouquet of flowers. Her anger dissipated immediately. So that's where the money had gone. She felt foolish for jumping to conclusions and almost ruining a special moment between them.

MIND READING AND MISINTERPRETATIONS

Many facts tend to get skewed with interpretations. Feelings left over from one interaction—not filtered or decompressed—can form the basis for many misinterpretations. External stressors also affect how you read into something, such as gridlock traffic on the way home or an awful day at work. What you personalize may in actuality be the remnant of an argument with a friend or a family member or your own swirling feelings of anxiety or inadequacy. These faulty interpretations can easily get projected elsewhere.

You cannot read each other's mind or just intrinsically understand one another's intentions. All takeaways, unless directly verbalized, can be mistakes in processing. Understanding your partner's underlying objective and thoughts at any given moment is virtually impossible, especially without slowing down your reactions until more information can provide you with much-needed clarity.

People largely operate on faulty beliefs, misunderstandings, and misinterpretations that will not get resolved without understanding and improving communication.

The biggest issue we see, as therapists, regarding communication is that couples simply don't have the right tools to get through these very necessary conversations. Without them, they are left to rely solely on the misinterpretations and faulty beliefs that will naturally rush in instead.

They exchange logistical information and complain about aspects of their partner's behaviors or choices, but they don't use effective and constructive dialogue. Instead of utilizing conversations to build understanding, most discussions revolve around day-to-day tasks and to-do lists. Couples may talk about work and the dog and gossip about friends, but they don't talk enough about their relationship, feelings, fears, hopes, themselves, or their needs. Communication is often not used as it should be—for resolution, for planning, and, in a general sense, for good. Discussions about the state of the relationship seem to be few and far between. When they do come up, it is usually within the context of a complaint or critique, which often plays a role in the avoidance of that topic next time around.

INFORMATION EXCHANGE
AND INDIGNATION

When dialogue between two people is nothing more than an information exchange, each party presents and defends their own position. This gets the air out but very often just leads both parties vying to top each other, in order to explain and justify their own positions. If couples do go as far as to address their core issues, it is often done in counterproductive and ineffective ways during times of agitation—usually with little repair afterward, making this subject taboo and downright scary.

Because such conversations do not always come naturally, it is easy to view them in a negative light, as a chore or an obligation. Most of us have been conditioned to fear these "we have to talk" conversations, as they usually revolve around negative topics. They are too often utilized to express disappointment, irritation, and anger, or to add more tasks to the already burdened infrastructure, which can quickly devolve into disagreements and animosity.

Communication this ineffective leads many couples to make every excuse in the book to avoid talking about needs and feelings. When the environment between you is filled with landmines, talking about emotions is not only uncomfortable, it makes you feel guarded. This leaves both parties feeling vulnerable and apprehensive.

Although couples feel hopeless when their relationship ends up here, collaborative communication and resolution is possible and doable. All it requires are a reframe and new tools that work to remove the bad and rebuild the good.

SOLUTIONS AND STRATEGIES

Removing the Bad: Collaborative Communication

When relationships encounter obstacles, whether external or internal, the only way to properly resolve these challenges is through a collaborative and calm, back-and-forth dialogue. This allows two people to present their individual perspectives, goals, and accompanying feelings authentically, and in the way that they mean it, with minimal defensiveness. Doing so creates a backdrop of ease and openness, thus facilitating the ability to work together to find a middle ground.

This collaboration must become the new normal, and through it, couples rid themselves of ineffective and conflict-driven discussions. It gets you back to the place where conversation flows between you, without the fear that every word has hidden meaning and accusation behind it.

Here are the necessary steps to make that a reality.

Baseline of Respect

Within the framework of better relationships, it is crucially important to hold your partner in high regard and operate from a foundation of respect and value. Addressing him or her kindly and respectfully opens dialogue lines and increases the desire to work together, which translates to better communication and allows for a more intimate back and forth that would be impossible as long as you insult and critique each other.

Showing one another respect by creating the space to discuss and communicate calmly should be the baseline from which to start the conversation. Having the commitment to address issues respectfully lays down the groundwork for learning to function as a team—one whose members support and enhance one another. To accomplish this, each partner needs to be able to take personal accountability of their own behavior.

OLIVIA & RON

Mini Corrections

Olivia was annoyed. She asked Ron to put the Amazon boxes away before her parents got there, and, as usual, there they were still on the floor. She marched to the backyard, intent on giving him a piece of her mind and then suddenly stopped. Olivia stood there for a second as she thought back to their couples counseling session earlier that week, where Ron talked to her about her tone and how disrespected he felt when she addressed him angrily. She felt conflicted for a second, wanting to berate him for forgetting, but she knew that was childish. She took a deep breath and holding herself back, she called out, "Hey, hon, my parents should be here soon. Please don't forget to grab those boxes."

Ron caught her eye and blew her a kiss. He made a point of dropping the task he was doing to go pick up the boxes. He knew his wife was trying, and he appreciated her attempt.

Listening and Accepting Your Different Perspectives

Having successful dialogue has to start with improving your ability to listen to one another with the goal of understanding, not just being understood.

Are you really listening, or just waiting to talk? When talking with your partner about your concerns, avoid just assuming that you know what is behind their actions or words. Let them speak and, as hard as it may be, work on yourself to learn to accept their viewpoint.

Remember that sometimes there are infinite versions of the truth based on our subjective interpretations. Your goal is not necessarily to convince the other person to see it your way or to agree with you, but rather to have them understand what you are saying and, conversely, to understand what they are saying. Once you have this dual understanding, you move toward finding solutions together.

Candor and Truth Telling

A better relationship requires the ability to be honest about its short-comings and the areas that need improvement. An inability to express how you feel is often the result of not wanting to hurt or offend. You may also feel that past attempts only led to counterattacks and conditioned you to stay silent. This may feel right in the moment, but these situations frequently just end up blowing up in your face.

JAKE & LYDIA

Honesty Helps

Jake avoided telling Lydia his feelings because he didn't want to hurt her. He didn't know how to tell her directly that he wanted space and found her neediness to be a turnoff. He was sure that it was her lack of friendships with other women that led her to minimize and even compete with his friendships. It was driving him crazy, and instead of being honest with her about his feelings so that she had an opportunity to do something about it, he kept it bottled up inside.

Lydia was aware of Jake's increased annoyance with her. She felt his growing disinterest in spending time with her and obviously didn't understand the subtext of his behavior. This led to her increased anxiety about the relationship, making her even more insistent that they spend time together. It led her to increase the nervous hovering that Jake hated. Lydia felt him moving away, so she moved closer, which just made him move farther away. The cyclical nature of this problem makes it unsolvable without honest dialogue.

While it is hard to give and accept negative feedback, we are so conflict-averse that we go out of our way to avoid any discussion that feels negative. Even if you are able to have these conversations, you often take a defensive stance, immediately ready to counterattack. This emotional avoidance of the hard stuff just works to make us way more emotionally fragile than we need to be. It leads us to be less capable, less competent in dealing with what life may throw our way. A happy life necessitates our ability to fix a problem as it arises, but that is wholly reliant on our ability to see and accept that the problem exists.

Most people use an array of defense mechanisms to avoid seeing themselves and their behaviors in an unfavorable light. Justifications, rationalizations, and a host of other defenses protect us from accepting actual truths. Because you don't or can't see yourself clearly, it is hard to accept these as facts when it comes from your partner.

However, as much as it may pain you both to hear negative feedback about you or your behavior, it is necessary that you work on your own sensitivity to allow this dialogue to take place. The partner who is delivering such a message should do so kindly, and softly, recognizing that it is not easy to accept negative feedback.

Openness and honesty must be nonnegotiable in marriage. It does not mean that you or your partner should say things callously and without regard for one another's vulnerabilities. The opposite is true. Being kind and forthcoming is crucial to your partner's ability to digest any constructive feedback. That means not holding back on what you are thinking and feeling but doing so gently without intent to wound.

Conveying these in an authentic and genuine manner and, conversely, managing your own defensiveness while you listen to your partner's feedback, even if it is negative, is crucial.

There is really no other choice, because, if ignored, little issues have the potential to snowball and become bigger issues. Addressing concerns before they fester and lead your relationship to further derail means becoming deliberate about fixing the problem through honesty.

Set Up "Talk Time"

Set aside weekly time for you two to talk. Schedule it regularly and make it a priority to use this time as an opportunity to elevate your relationship, creating a safe space for you to address your issues instead of silently suffering, or bombarding each other with constant concerns. Timing is important—so have these talks when there are minimal stressors coming in from other sources. The time should be free of distractions so you can both be fully present. Turn off the TV and cell phones, put the kids to bed, and concentrate on one another.

Use this time to heal your relationship from the damage and hits it has taken. All in all, this is a positive activity that can greatly improve your life and feelings for one another. Be serious yet optimistic when you get to the discussion table, as your attitude and mindset will have an impact on its success.

A hopeful and positive attitude can mend the mistakes made in unresolved past transgressions. Start your discussions by acknowledging the positive attempts made by your partner in the previous week, noting what was productive, what you liked, and what felt good.

Rules of Engagement

Success within "talk time" necessitates establishing some ground rules and boundaries to get on the same page and avoid slipping into the same unproductive patterns of communication. Discuss what rules need to be set. The goal is to eliminate any negative discourse that in the past would lead you to stop and give up. Maybe your partner has a habit of cutting you off before you are done speaking, or maybe you have a tendency to storm out of the room when the talk gets heated. Rules force you to refrain from bad habits and create good ones that won't sabotage the conversation. Setting time aside at the beginning of your discussion to compliment and address the progress is a good example of such a rule.

Protect these discussions from old and inadequate patterns through use of a code word or phrase that is intended as a stopping measure. Use this code word/phrase to take a time-out if you have to, in case talk time escalates to a place where discussions are no longer productive and the anger momentarily rebounds. (See more on the code word/phrase in chapter 5.) Doing so will stop the cycle of decline and allow you to finally move forward in practicing more fruitful communication.

In our practice we suggest saying something shocking or ridiculous like, "We need more purple starfish," or "Man, this Chinese food is salty." Make sure that whatever phrase you choose is unrelated to any past conflict and is not just a simple prompt to "stop" or "not now," which can easily further inflame or trigger the other person. The reason these familiar words won't work as code words is that they are usually your go-to word or phrase, one that has been connected to unsuccessful resolutions in the past. Most likely your partner doesn't trust that these responses will lead to good resolution. It is often seen as a brush-off, which blocks your partner's need to get it out.

Embrace this code word as a safeguard to this new dialogue as it also acts as a signifier to your mutual commitment to honor and cultivate the marriage.

Verbal and Nonverbal Messages

Your words and body language matter. Use your discussions to understand how specific comments, words, body language, and other nonverbal cues directly impact your interactions and could take matters south (such as rolling your eyes, raising your voice, or constantly checking your phone).

Day-to-Day Talks

Other than talk time, be mindful of the day-to-day discussions you have. Make an attempt for these to be more interesting and deeper than the usual conversations of just recounting your day. If you find yourself racking your brain to find topics to discuss with one another, here are some fun ways you could jump-start your conversations:

Talking Jar: Find an empty jar and place it in a convenient location near some paper and pens. Throughout the week, jot down open-ended questions or ideas for conversations and place them folded inside the jar. Don't overthink it. These could be silly or serious. Then when you have some time to talk, you can randomly select a folded scrap and use its content as a jumping-off point to get to know each other better and to encourage conversations of more than just the shared life.

Question-Related Books/Games: If you don't want to come up with the topics yourself, explore the many excellent tools at your disposal to elevate your conversations to the next level, such as Table Topics, a conversation starter tool that can help jump-start interesting dialogue. You can and should use an aid if you find yourself at a loss about what to say to one another. Books or games can provide creative ways to facilitate engaging and personal conversations that are outside the framework of regular surface-level discussions.

Rebuilding the Good: Constructing a Safety Net

Use the resources available to provide a safer environment to engage one another in activities that trigger happier outcomes. Having positive discussions that have nothing to do with the "issues" can help fortify your ability to talk. Progress may be slow, but as long as communication is moving in the right direction, see it as positive and much-needed growth.

Filling in the Blanks

Remember that you do not have the ability to read each other's mind. Even if you know each other well, it still does not mean that you can ever guess what your mate is thinking or feeling at any given moment. Telling your spouse something like "you think" or "you believe" is just the projection of your own assumptions.

In your attempts to right some entrenched wrongs, it is crucial that you give your partner both the benefit of the doubt and the opportunity to respond *before* you forge on with your own interpretation.

Learn to Separate the Behavior from the Person

Extrapolating a singular problem into a pattern and weaving isolated mistakes into general issues devalues and undercuts your partner. This is done through the use of *always* and *never*, which are usually not only incorrect, but they fail to recognize what your partner does provide, and thus serve as a negative reinforcer.

For example, Steve sees a rake left in the front yard. Annoyed that it was not put away yet again, he walks in the door and greets Anne with a critique: "C'mon! You just left the rake outside, again. I've really had it with you leaving my tools outside. You *never* put anything back in its spot." This is an exaggeration that is simply not fair to make—especially as Anne could easily point out that it is also not true. Conversely, she has many examples that would indicate otherwise. But that just leaves both parties engaged in a pointless back and forth of subjective opinions.

Move from the all-or-nothing extremes of *always* and *never* to the more infrequent *sometimes* or *occasionally*. This helps you both understand that a person *does* do the things you wish them not to do, but that there are some occasions where this *doesn't* happen, and it is not personal. You can still let your partner know about your disappointment or hurt regarding the existence or absence of a behavior, without condemning their intent or value.

Retracting and Reframing

You and your partner will make mistakes. Instead of immediately reacting, bring it to their attention and allow them the space to take it back, do an about-face, and correct. Remember that at this point there are still bad habits built into your dynamic. This step will allow you to eradicate and replace these habits. Instead of blame or anger, try responses like these: "That was uncalled for. Can you say it differently?" or "I am sure you didn't mean it that way, but that hurt my feelings, babe. Will you try again?"

Spinning the Bad to the Good

Learn to reframe a negative into a positive, focusing less on the complaint and more on the true desire from which it stems. For instance, when Lori saw Gunther's clothes nicely folded on the bed, while hers remained on the couch unfolded, she lost it: "Can't you ever take care of me? You are so selfish." This could be reframed into a positive if Lori would say, "Thanks for washing our clothes, but next time could you fold mine as well? It would be a great help, because sometimes they get wrinkled once out of the dryer."

When the expressed need is delivered rather than the complaint, you will get better results.

LIZZIE & DAVE

Meeting of Minds

Lizzie made plans for her and her husband, Dave, for a night out with their friends on Friday at 6:00 p.m. When Dave found out, he got upset and lashed out. His anger flared, as meeting that early wouldn't allow him to get home and change first. Reacting negatively, and assuming that Lizzie set the earlier time as a self-serving move because she prefers to eat early, created a negative interaction.

Spinning this into a positive, Dave could have thanked her for taking the initiative to make plans, and then asked if she would push the meet time to a little later in the evening, as he would prefer to drive with her and get a little extra time together.

Clarifying

Without check-ins and clarifications, events and words can get easily misinterpreted, leading you to see each other through the wrong lens—which allows for resentment to build. When in doubt about something you heard, make it a habit to check in and clarify. It can be as simple as asking, "This is what I heard. Is that what you meant?"

Remember to let each other speak freely. Don't interrupt or jump into their dialogue. Instead, jot down what you want to address and cycle back to it when it is your time to speak. Talk about what you could do differently. Through clarifying instead of immediately reacting, you learn once again to give your mate the benefit of the doubt.

ADDITIONAL TALK TIME STRATEGIES

Reminisce

Too often, couples tend to focus on past mistakes or what they perceive to not be going well in the present. With Married Roommates, it is especially easy to focus on the day-to-day tasks and notice what we find to be missing and unfulfilling.

Taking time to reminisce about the positives—the moments and attributes that led to "I do"—is important. You can learn from your past in many ways. It can be the missing key to remembering what you used to love about one another, activities you used to enjoy together, and ways you used to avoid negativity and conflict.

Plan an evening of reminiscing by pulling out old photos and mementos of your early years together. Perhaps open a bottle of wine, put on some nostalgic music, and let the past take you away from your current feelings. Talk about your history. Laugh over past moments that you had all but forgotten. Think about what you used to like about one another and what you used to do together. Try to remember what you were drawn and attracted to. Did you call each other any pet names or share silly banter?

Use this night to revive these memories and be intentional about them. You are still those same people underneath.

List the Likes

With the amount of stress that couples struggle through, great moments from our past can be forgotten and discarded, as if they never happened. Couples need to be more deliberate in remembering the good times in their relationship and each other.

Use this talk time strategy to tell each other and at the same time remind yourself of all the good things about your partner. Take the time to make a list of ten positive attributes of the other person—a favorite characteristic, an attractive trait, or even a fond memory. Then take turns running down your list and remark how your partner being this way makes you feel.

Copy the list into your phone or journal—any place you can cycle back to frequently to remind yourself of why you want to work on your marriage. See this as akin to practicing daily gratitude. The twist is that the gratitude is solely geared to work on your ability to value and appreciate your partner. Remind yourself of what you are thankful for and see as valuable within your spouse.

Chart Your Hopes

When you first got together, you probably had so many dreams and goals that you wanted to achieve together. Through the years and hardships, these can disappear from sight. It is definitely time to bring them back. Couples can have difficulty having hope, as they don't know how to feel more optimistic about their future.

More than anything, we would encourage you to work together to make your marriage a place where you can open up and still share your hopes and dreams—a safe place where you can once again be vulnerable with one another. This will bring about a deeper friend-ship that will sustain the relationship when times are tough and conflict runs high.

Walk It Out

Taking a walk together can sometimes be a safer and more produc-tive way to converse. The absence of direct eye contact in a parallel conversation helps people speak more freely. Not looking at one another can avoid the self-censorship that you may impose on yourself when picking up on your partner's reactive nonverbal cues. It allows you to be more authentic and less judgmental of yourself *and* your partner.

When we prescribe these walks to our clients, we encourage them to establish ground rules that specify off-limit subjects such as work, kids, friends, family, house, politics, movies, or news. It takes the easy, usual go-to and safe subjects off the table. These restric-tions force couples to refocus on the relationship and better identify the items that are missing in their life. This can start out as a weekly walk and increase to multiple times a week and even nightly.

This time together can be a reprieve from the duties and responsibilities that typically drain authentic discussions. It can help couples understand each other better—initially by tapping into and identifying what brings them both happiness, and then by collaborating on ways to bring these qualities into the relationship.

The Power of a Venting Moment

There are times when you are upset about a variety of things unrelated to your partner. It could be as a result of your boss's or clients' demands, traffic, power struggles with your kids, or a fight with a friend or family member. People often carry these outside frustrations and easily project them into their relationships, as it is generally a safer target. This is not done intentionally. Being aware of the negative impact our environment can have on us helps couples develop the insight to seek out healthier ways to let go of their stress.

We often recommend couples practice a "venting moment" to get rid of these struggles and frustrations effectively. Since you are often each other's sole support system, provide one another with a five-minute free pass to vent about outside stressors, where you solely listen. Resist offering any feedback, suggestions, advice, or input. It is a cathartic way to be there for one another without trying to fix things or take each other's stress personally. This offers the struggling party a way to let go of external stressors, not unfairly project them onto their mate. Ultimately, venting moments help unite the two against all problems, as friends.

What happens when real communication is hijacked and manifests as escalating conflict? In the next chapter, we will explore couples stuck in negative cycles of resentment and distrust, which manifests as scorekeeping, tit for tats, and low blows.

CHAPTER 4

KEY TAKEAWAYS

✔ Communication is difficult for couples. They get caught up in faulty assumptions and misinterpretations, often mistaking poor intentions with poor outcomes.

✔ Because communication is the only tool at your disposal to navigate your differences and understand one another, it is crucial you learn how to communicate effectively.

✔ Your shared life will require compromise, and the negotiation will not be easy.

✔ People are incredibly complex. Truth is often a subjective interpretation depending on the lens with which you view it. The way your brain interprets stimuli and makes connections is not always based in fact or grounded in reality.

✔ People don't think or process their world in the same way—unless you know someone's internal dialogue, you cannot assume to know the complexities behind even the simplest interaction.

✔ Couples often have a lot of surface-level interactions, but they don't go deep enough to discuss their emotional relationship, feelings, fears, and hopes.

✔ Communication must be a calm, collaborative back and forth that is stopped via code word when escalated. A baseline of respect and positive regard is necessary for us to open up and allow for vulnerability.

✔ Remember it's not just what we say but our silent nonverbals and what they are saying regarding the value of your partner.

✔ Being honest is not easy, but it is necessary to grow past the resentments and walls you've built.

✔ Practice the use of communication strategies consistently.

5

CONFLICTS AND COMBAT

Critiques and Criticisms

Jordan rolled her eyes in response to JP's diatribe about the dishes. She knew it drove him crazy when the dishes piled up in the sink, but that was the way she had always done it prior to their moving in together. Honestly, she had bigger fish to fry.

It annoyed her that during her busiest workdays, she still had to conform and do it his way. Being ex-military left him pretty rigid about household duties in a way she didn't appreciate. It felt controlling. Every time he lectured her about tidiness, she felt like a failing '50s housewife and, even worse, that she had moved in with her dad. Her dad used to chastise and berate her mom about the household duties; it was all she heard growing up. When JP asked why she didn't just do the dishes, it upset her to the core. Instead of telling him what upset her, she usually responded by making snide, sarcastic remarks about his rigidity.

JP hated the way Jordan rolled her eyes when she disagreed with him. It seemed like common sense that the dishes should be done regularly, but with Jordan it felt like his requests fell on deaf ears. This became a major source of contention in the past few months as she increasingly got more comfortable and, sadly, messier with all aspects of their home. He found himself making daily comments or, admittedly, even slightly passive-aggressive digs when he came home from a long day of work only to see the dishes that had accumulated since the afternoon. It triggered many of their fights.

For JP this conflict went deeper than just the dishes. It was about respect and love. As the oldest child of a single mom, he had stepped up and taken on the household responsibilities to make it easier on his mom, so she didn't have more to do when she finally shuffled in exhausted from her long workday. He had loved to see her face light up when she saw a clean kitchen, dinner started, or even the beds made.

His early home life is not something he opened up about with Jordan, as it seemed like a given that she should just understand. Not only didn't she get it but she doubled down on her disrespect, demeaning and humiliating him. The name calling, insinuating he acted like her dad, or that this was just a part of some sort of unhealthy military inflexibility hurt and took his frustration to new levels. He found himself engaged in a tit for tat, punishing her in other ways for not understanding his needs. Lately he had even been wondering if he should just end it, despite the otherwise strong connection they shared.

DISAGREEING IS NORMAL

Some conflict in relationships is inevitable, for there are many times when two people's differing opinions and/or needs will clash and run counter to one another. Legitimate and illegitimate sources of irritability and disapproval will inevitably lead to disappointment and dispute. This is normal, and is to be expected, especially in marriage, when many times you do not get an individual vote.

While some disagreements are unavoidable in relationships—because let's face it, you are not always going to see things eye-to-eye—there are those Married Roommates who cannot move past the problem to a solution. They cycle around obstacles and hurdles, blaming each other, holding grudges, instead of actually taking on the problem. As a result, they frequently fall into patterns of bickering, even over the most insignificant things.

These roommates often live in a tenuous reality—nitpicking, pointing fingers, and finding fault with one another over many decisions and choices. Instead of finding common ground and letting some things go, they exist in a daily reality where a competitive tit for tat is the norm. Couples who consistently hem and haw, split hairs, and insist on getting the last word in create systemic bad habits. Getting upset and angry with one another allows you to blow off steam, which in the short term intensifies the conflict, but in the long term weakens your connection. It creates an unsafe environment for important and needed negotiation, which is unnecessary and damaging to the core of the relationship.

Couples can jab each other in endless ways and consistently hit below the belt. Perhaps they are not even aware that by egging each other on, making snarky comments, or being petty or mean they are just cementing this dynamic and ensuring that this poor behavior goes on indefinitely. At some point, it just becomes a retaliatory cycle.

These poor habits boomerang back and forth and only up the ante. It gets to the point that you can flip out for something as petty as the toothpaste cap being off.

People are imperfect. Everyone makes mistakes or has traits or behaviors that create a neighborhood of glass houses. By overreacting, you both create a poor pattern where you learn to work against each other. Blaming, shaming, mocking, or simply refusing to see or accept one another's points or reasoning only undermines the relationship, as it always comes back to bite us in the rear.

Conditioning one another to go to battle creates a day-to-day reality entrenched in hostility and defensiveness. Altercations over the smallest things can get to alarming and usually uncontrollable places in what seems like an instant.

Negative interactions build on themselves and escalate. Usually the underlying problem in these combustible situations are long-standing, unresolved needs, which have become entangled in pain, fear, and hopelessness. They may be triggered by what seem like insignificant matters, but those seemingly small triggers are generally always tied back to a larger core issue, which is the loss of the emotional bond and the struggling and overwhelmed functional relationship. Avoidance of too many core issues is how you became roommates in the first place.

ELLIOT & AVA

Competitive Scorekeeping

Elliot parked his car in the allotted space in their apartment complex. Knowing that they would be using his car for the long trip to his parents the next day, he made a point of cleaning the clutter and old cups that had been stacking up for the past week.

Admittedly, he was a bit of a slob, but he usually took the effort to clean the mess before Ava got in his car. He threw most of it out in the downstairs bin before heading upstairs to their apartment but thought twice before throwing in the almost full Starbucks cup from earlier that day, not wanting to give the building's cleaners more work to do.

When he walked in, Ava took one look at the Starbucks cup and gave him a dirty look. "Just another example of what a selfish prick you are," she said, eyes focused accusingly on the cup.

"What are you talking about?" Elliott asked, confused by her hostility.

"You got yourself a coffee but, as usual, didn't even think of me," she said. "You know what? Why don't you just go to your parents alone then. I'm done."

In an instant, they were at each other's throats, screaming at one another and crossing red lines. Ava felt justified to talk about Elliot's parents, becoming demeaning and disrespectful. Elliot spiraled right along with her, calling Ava a "crazy, low-class bitch."

The fight ended when he stormed out and went to see his parents on his own, but the nastiness and disrespect they showed each other continued for days afterward, neither recognizing or understanding the other's hurt, which was underlying the anger and frustration. Ava had already been on edge about their visit to his family's house, which always ended in a fight when he failed to stand up to his dad, who was consistently condescending toward her. Elliot got upset because it seemed that Ava always tried to get out of the visits with his parents by coming up with the same tired old argument that seemed to conveniently forget all the times that he stood up for her.

EXPLOSIVE FIGHTS AND ESCALATIONS

In some relationships, it seems as though any difference of opinion—
no matter how slight—can cause explosive fights, and these escalations eventually become an everyday occurrence. Issues that other
couples can resolve easily become roadblocks for those roommates
who are entrenched in this pattern. Even conversations that start
off friendly enough can quickly devolve to a heated and escalated
place. Misunderstandings and differing opinions are easily misinterpreted as personal attacks or critiques and then used as the basis
or defense for the subsequent counterattack. It's almost as if people
already have their finger on the trigger.

These attacks do not allow couples to see each other's true pain.
The combative dynamic that some Married Roommates allow for
creates a destructive undercurrent that teams one against the other,
affecting *everything* else that is going on.

ESCALATION TRIGGERS FIGHT OR FLIGHT

When couples go from zero to sixty over what appear to be the
smallest of things, they hurl accusations, threats, names, and even
curse at each other. Unfortunately, during those moments, your
own physiology works against you, as escalation hijacks your ability
to communicate effectively by setting off your fight-or-flight instinct.

The fight-or-flight instinct is your body's evolutionary alarm
system kicking in. Your brain triggers this response in order to
protect you from what it perceives as a threat. Whether there is
real danger lurking around is irrelevant to this instinctual reaction. The material for all this combustion originates from hurt and
hopelessness—all normal, acceptable feelings that instantly erupt
into intense anger or rage in an escalated situation.

Once sparked, the reaction simply turns on without your control or even awareness. You may feel your muscles tense and heart rate going up. Your chest might palpitate or your palms may become clammy. Other symptoms may be a tense neck, warm forehead, itchy shoulders or skin, arrested breathing, watery and barely blinking eyes, shaky limbs, and an inability to sit still—all physiological signs that your body is getting you ready to deal with this threat.

As your body reacts, your cognitive brain is put on standby. "You" seemingly have no control of what happens next. Once the brain has assessed danger, the red emergency light comes on, furiously blinking as internally the brain prepares for the threat by shutting down all nonessential functions to deal with the oncoming problem. It does so by increasing the bodily functions that will aid the fight-or-flight response. It releases certain hormones such as adrenaline and cortisol to increase your heart rate and blood pressure, boosting energy and glucose supplies in the bloodstream.

During this time the cognitive brain—our thinking apparatus—is not in control, which can lead you to act irrationally and destructively. When in the grips of a fight-or-flight moment, you are not physiologically capable of talking calmly. The nonessential departments that the brain just turned off are the very ones needed to understand, empathize, and resolve. So, while in this state, the dialogue between two people usually does not go well, because it cannot.

Unfortunately, when you escalate in an argument with your partner, when assessing this danger, your brain doesn't account for the fact that you love this person and do not really want to hurt them. In that moment they are *a threat to your survival*, and you will do whatever is necessary to survive.

The fight-or-flight instinct is not exclusive to your partner. The very same symptoms could be triggered at work, by another customer in a store, by road rage, or by a condescending hotel clerk. Just as easily, it could flare up by your brother, a close friend, an old coworker, or your parents. Your unique physiological reactions will play out in the same ways, in all arenas where you are prompted into this state.

With your partner, such triggers may happen more frequently and can be more personal and more hostile because the event is usually connected to a much deeper hurt, resentment, or dissatisfaction. Because you perceive one another as adversaries, while your intellectual abilities are hijacked, all bets are off. There will be no safety, or love. You easily become two animals that will utilize whatever is at your disposal to disarm the threat. You may take stories told in confidence about families, past relationships, or mistakes and hurl them at each other. Using the most hurtful insecurities to now open up multiple fronts of attack, you interrupt and cut each other off, become defensive or sarcastic, and use words that intend to defend or hurt rather than heal. You use generalities and absolutes, like *never* and *always*, to attack and counterattack.

The battle can be brutal.

It is extremely important to understand what happens in the human body when fight or flight is triggered so that you can avoid inflicting greater damage on each other and your relationship. Having an intellectual awareness of the internal systems that control your behavior and response is crucial to eliminating the escalation that ends up destroying your partnership.

MARC & STELLA

You Always and You Never

Every time they spoke it felt like a tit for tat, where each of them aimed to win at all cost. Marc knew he was now as much to blame for their drag-out fights, but it felt like he had to adopt her style of fighting because Stella would never hear him otherwise. Stella constantly brought up her disappointment with his shortcomings. Her critique hurt him more than she could ever imagine. While he could do more to contribute, his everyday efforts went largely unnoticed. Tonight Stella had all but called herself a single mom, despite his having done this week's grocery shopping, volunteering at the school, handling the dentist, setting up playdates, and getting both kids to soccer practice on time.

He used to just take it, because he didn't want to fight, but she just got more demeaning and explosive when he remained quiet. It was almost like she didn't hear him until he got aggressive and combative. When she walked in earlier and saw the kids' homework all over the kitchen counter, she flew into a rage. "You couldn't even put their homework away? What the fuck, Marc?" Stella's tone rose with each syllable. "Why must I always do everything in this house?" she shouted as she angrily shuffled through the homework. She left the kitchen still visibly angry, got to the bedroom, and slammed the door behind her.

Stella was fuming as she lay on the bed. It just wasn't fair that he made her out to be the bad guy. Becoming a mom had really overwhelmed her and caught her off guard. She found the pressures of navigating other people's lives difficult to manage successfully. Having two kids to take care of, as well as a childlike husband, was aggravating. Marc was helpful at times but also a slacker. She had done so much research on the importance of quality family time, and while he seemed to intuitively get it, the behaviors never seemed to change. She had been on him to start a family hike tradition on Saturdays, but he dropped it. She wanted a family game night, but he dropped it. Asking for an electronics-free dinner table seemed more than reasonable, but apparently that was too much for him.

She wanted to calmly talk about her concerns, because she truly felt like she was drowning, but it never came out that way. Within seconds, they were at it, screaming, accusing, and cursing at one another in the most awful ways. Their kids bore witness to the hateful tsunami between them. She had said some pretty horrible things tonight, and while she sort of felt justified, she also felt really bad.

As she took a deep breath, her face softened. He actually did more than she was giving him credit for. It's not that he did nothing, or that she even followed through herself consistently, if she was truly honest. She just wanted him to participate and sometimes take the lead more than he did.

CLASHING REACTIVITY

Everyone responds to the fight-or-flight instinct differently. For some, that may be defending or withdrawing, while for others, it looks more like attacking and decimating. One partner may be overly aggressive and vocal, telling it like it is, or at least how they see it, while the other shuts down after repeatedly requesting, even begging, the other to stop.

Although the flight partner's natural instinct may be to run from the danger, if the fight partner does not relent and continues to try to explain, defend, or seek out the now impossible resolution, the conflict will bring out the fighter in both of them. In much the same way that if you corner an animal, you force it to attack. That's what will happen with even the most benign partner, and the conflict becomes a recipe for disaster.

DEBORAH & RAUL

Every Day, All Day

Deborah couldn't believe Raul's nerve. Running a business was hard enough, but running it with her husband was much more challenging than she had expected. She still had two marketing meetings to attend, and then she would have to swing by the grocery store for dinner. Raul knew how much she struggled with the business taxes. They had bitter fights about that very issue, and, once again, he dumped it on her lap at the last minute. She felt so overwhelmed that she was barely functioning. Her frustration with Raul had been increasing all week.

When she saw the text from him asking her to deal with the insurance company, which he had promised to take care of, her anger bubbled over. She couldn't contain her rage, especially since tonight was his weekly poker night with his buddies. Her mind cycled with the unfairness of his lighter schedule, his inconsistencies, and her contempt of him.

When Raul popped his head into her office, her face must have betrayed her fierce anger, and naturally he picked a fight. Another fight. They seemed to be having them every other day now. It made both their home and office uncomfortable, tension-ridden environments.

Raul picked up on Deborah's mood instantly. She had the self-righteous martyr look she'd inherited from her mother. Her body language clearly indicated what would happen next. She would hurl an enraged litany of complaints at him about how she does more, feels more tired, and is less happy. He heard about this almost every day. Deborah felt like she did more on a daily basis, but he wholeheartedly disagreed. He took on his share of the responsibilities both at home and at work. He just didn't complain and rage about it incessantly.

She seemed to forget how much he took on for her—all the favors and schedule changes he would make, no questions asked. Although he did insist on his downtime, she did not. Deborah was like a machine. She could just keep working without having fun, and he just wasn't built like that.

When they first started the business together, it was great, but now, even though they had the best fiscal year ever, he constantly felt trapped and invalidated. He was so sick of it. Sometimes he even hated her for it.

Although many Married Roommates equate conflict and fighting with communication, it is crucial to reframe their thinking to understand that the minute an interchange between two people escalates, the ability to understand each other or empathize goes away. When the dynamic is anything except calm, even when you think that you are listening, your mind is busy, swirling with activity as it forges on to formulate your retort, by poking holes in theirs. You do so because you want to defend yourself and justify your own behavior.

It is too easy to go further and escalate into combat mode. Once there, neither party is capable of empathy, which is ultimately what you both want. What you get instead is a fiery back and forth, where you do not allow one another to complete the presentation of their point before you hotly debate it.

It is difficult to hold a conversation with, much less express yourself to, a person who shuts down in anger and resentment or becomes defensive and emotional. Although you may endlessly keep trying to appeal to their logic or emotion, if your tone or body language comes off a certain way, many times the other person shuts down (or more likely escalates further, igniting a firestorm). They are no longer present in the discussion.

Couples can become stuck in a cycle of hurt and victimization that is never resolved. Unfortunately, every partner who feels like a victim has another partner who feels the exact same way. The pattern pits you against one another, ensuring that you will continue to use destructive methods of attack or protection instead of effective communication that involves listening or acknowledging contributions.

THE UNRESOLVED AFTERMATH

Regardless of your personal combat style, fight or flight creates a setting where you both lose by continuously wounding one another through devastating allegations, tone, and a slew of other reactions, which can be extreme and detrimental.

What you say and do while in this state can and will be vicious. It may be what you feel in that moment, but usually it's not what you mean. While seeing red, you will say and do things that you later regret, once your cognitive brain is back in control.

Unfortunately, the caustic remarks that come out of you while in this state inflict the biggest cuts and hurtful damage to your relationship. Our clients frequently cite the words said or done in fight or flight as damning evidence of what their partner really feels. Although the guilty party may be highly regretful, apologizing frequently often does not heal the damage.

Because these couples can't talk effectively, where this defensive posturing exists, communication will always stumble and fail, making the main focus shift to the reactiveness, again leaving the door wide open for continued conflict.

It's a maddening, frustrating pattern, yet many Married Roommates seem incapable of getting past this cyclical way of attacking one another, because they fall into the trap of igniting the fight-or-flight response. Once you understand that what you say and do while in this state is so incredibly destructive, it should motivate you to avoid such conflict.

RICH & SHARI

It's Never Good Enough

Rich sat and watched the game for the first time in what seemed like weeks. He had knocked off all the errands on the list Shari gave him, hitting up Costco and Home Depot in record time. He even returned two of Shari's purchases to Nordstrom and filled both cars with gas. It had been a long Saturday, but he was proud of himself for getting everything done and was excited to finally unwind and relax.

While he didn't usually expect a thank-you, Shari burst into anger and started yelling when she looked in the Home Depot bag he had handed her. So he forgot a few things. How could

*batteries and light bulbs be such a big deal, especially with
everything else he successfully accomplished? Her disrespectful
comments cut him to the core and made him feel like an
incompetent child, one who couldn't get anything right.*

■

*Shari was furious. It had been two weeks since she had told
Rich to take care of the outdoor lights, and he kept promising
he would. Their daughter's crib soother was out of batteries,
and the fan remote still didn't work despite her polite efforts
to ask him to get to it, and her not-so-subtle cues. Now they
had guests coming over tonight, and the outdoor space would
feel like crap. It had been muggy and the fan played such a
key role for their comfort, which she had emphasized to Rich
time and time again. She hated to be a nag—and it always
seemed to get him upset—but he was bringing out the worst
in her. Shari couldn't understand why Rich couldn't just do
things right away instead of procrastinating and waiting to
the last minute. It fueled her anxiety, sometimes leading to
disproportionate anger.*

*Shari didn't want to be his "parent." Always telling him what
to do was tedious and annoying. She never used to be like this,
but as life became more difficult, she had to be. If she didn't
notice and remember the dozens of things that had to be taken
care of on a daily basis, he never would. She felt alone as the
only responsible adult, always terrified that she would forget
something, and that the house of cards would come crashing
down on them if she wasn't holding It up. She knew that she
shouldn't curse and call him names, but he made her so angry.*

UNRESOLVED ISSUES

The aftermath of these intense, negative interactions leaves both parties hurt, often feeling emotionally battered and bruised. Angry and deeply wounded, both parties usually choose to stay away from each other for hours or even days following these conflicts. You hope for an apology, or at least for the light bulb of remorse to go off in your partner, but it rarely comes right away, *if ever.*

While eventually you do calm down, because both of you are left wounded, you often walk on eggshells afterward to avoid a possible redo. Unfortunately, outside of "I am sorry," most couples never take back those destructive words said during escalation. Not cycling back to mend these issues allows for negative interpretations to take hold. In our practice we refer to this as "cementing the narrative."

Many couples reengage timidly, going for safer topics such as the kids, work, their friends, politics, or celebrity gossip than the issue behind the fight. They distract themselves through mutual TV watching and lighter subjects about other people's problems. These are definitely safer topics, but because their interpersonal issues remain unresolved, these sensitive topics can easily find their way back into conversations. Even those discussions that start off innocently enough can somehow trigger past issues.

While this eggshell-walk temporarily keeps the peace by allowing the intensity of the conflict to fade away, when the hurts and echoes of these moments don't get discussed or resolved in any meaningful way, they merely lie dormant until the next go-around. Ignoring the elephant in the room doesn't actually deal with the problem, just kicks it down the road, where it only remains out of sight until conflict is triggered again.

In fact, pushing the problem away to an unseen place ultimately makes the conflict worse. While it may help in the moment, in actuality avoidance helps to create a nasty feedback loop of neg-ativity, where every fight and disagreement holds the potential to uncork all the dormant, out-of-sight ones.

For the larger foundational issues between a couple, benign triggers can manifest everywhere, at any time. The unresolved issues can bubble up to the surface in our day-to-day interac-tions in many verbal and nonverbal ways. The longer you don't deal with it, the quicker a problem will surface. Hurt from pre-vious fights can act as an accelerant, adding fuel to the fire of all future disagreements, blowing them up to enormous dimensions. Avoidance sets you up for more fights and more hurt, continuing in a never-ending cycle of current problems unearthing unre-solved past issues.

Despite the deep regret and hurt that you both may feel from previous crippling encounters, they tend to follow the same course time and time again, further inciting the problem but never really reaching the solution.

Bringing up the past and cycling around unresolved issues is an unfortunate way of life for many couples. Whether it is a bat-tle of wills or pride that keeps your genuine understanding and empathy for one another at bay, or just an overall failure to work more cohesively together as a team, is irrelevant. The outcome is always hopelessness.

BATTLE-WEARY AVOIDANCE

Failing to get your needs met because communication is ineffective is a bitter pill to swallow. When all attempts to talk lead to explo-sive anger or emotional shutdown, couples eventually grow tired and wary of fighting, and most shut down and give up.

Living together obviously complicates issues, as you are inexplicably tied together. It is not easy to run away and get some alone time when you must face each other at every turn of the hallway.

As you disengage, conflicts may become more infrequent, but more toxic and hurtful when they do occur. Until issues are dealt with, small triggers linked to the larger unresolved issues will cause a constant state of instability and irritability. Once realization and finally acceptance that change will not occur sets in, you shut down, withdrawing emotionally. You start to avoid all unnecessary interactions, drawing inward and slowly pulling away.

BARBARA & DEVIN

Dormant Conflicts

Barbara had always been frustrated with the roommate status of her domestic life. She felt suffocated by the very fact that every weeknight was the same drill, and the weekend followed the same uninspiring routine. They didn't have kids, and that was a mutual decision, but her reason behind this was the freedom and adventure she had always wanted to have in her life.

Devin was a great guy in most ways, but he never made plans. They never went out to dinner unless she planned it, and the number of trips they had taken over their six years of marriage could be counted on one hand. Money was not the issue, as they had a beautiful home, nice cars, and the latest toys, but she felt empty and lost without having anything to do or plan for.

She had tried over the years to articulate her needs to Devin. In the beginning it was communicated as lighthearted suggestions, which grew over time to become outright demands. Her patience withered over the years, and she produced a snappy tone with Devin. The resulting conflict between them went in two ways. Her scorekeeping list of everything he was doing or, rather, not doing resulted in an exchange of hateful words and culminated in their not speaking for days on end. During the more extreme episodes, she would go so far as to put their marriage on the line or demand couples counseling. Then he would pacify her with a two-week change only to go back to his baseline behavior. This behavior went on for years until eventually she just gave up. Her interest in him declined and their interactions became more cursory.

After nine months without conflict, Barbara casually told Devin about her coworker's new boyfriend and the romantic trip to Paris that they had just returned from. Devin knew her coworker well, and so Barbara expected Devin to ask more about the new boyfriend or the trip, but instead he blew up and stormed into the other room. When Barbara was talking about Paris, all he heard was her ongoing persistence and unhappiness about their lack of travel. It brought back all the fights and arguments about what he didn't give her, and what she found lacking in him. She had forgotten and given up on their old, unresolved conflict, but he had not.

In our practice, we see huge eruptions over a coffee, a \$3 expenditure, or being five minutes late. In isolation, these annoyances are small and inconsequential, but in the bigger context of long, enduring, and painful conflicts, they represent tipping points to larger unresolved issues that were swept under the rug for too long a time.

ERIKA & JAY

Transitional Impacts

Jay had always been close to his family. Because they lived nearby, he got to spend a large amount of time with them. Since getting pregnant and having their son last year, Erika had taken less and less of an interest in being around Jay's family. She rarely accepted an invitation to join their get-togethers, and she was reluctant to let him take the baby there by himself.

Erika was disappointed with her in-laws. Although they were never rude directly, they were not helpful. She felt they did not really like her, so she stopped going. She justified her behavior by rationalizing that she just had a baby and was overwhelmed.

While the baby was a joy, there was always so much work to do and never enough time to do it. Between work and taking care of the baby, she was indeed exhausted. Erika was running ragged. She felt alone as Jay took a more secondary role in parenting, because he was always at his parents' house.

It was a frequent argument between them, and despite fighting about it almost weekly, they still didn't see eye-to-eye. She felt that he didn't take his responsibilities as a father and husband seriously. He came home late from work every night and still did the same things he did before the baby, like spending hours playing video games with his cousins and getting drunk at his mom's house every weekend.

Erika interpreted his constant need to be with his family as him not wanting to spend time with her and the baby. Because she felt rejected, Erika responded by attacking Jay verbally. From her perspective, she made Jay and their son her top priority. She worked, cleaned, paid the bills, cooked their food, and took care of the house. It didn't seem like she was asking that much of Jay, considering everything she carried on her plate. It was infuriating to her that Jay couldn't put their family first and have some boundaries with his own family. It made her feel as if he didn't care, that she was in this thing alone.

Jay loved his son but parenthood did not impact him in the same way it did for Erika. She wanted to spend every single moment together bonding, excluding his own parents in the process. Her refusal to join family gatherings was now a point of contention in their relationship, a trigger point that led to arguments and escalated misunderstandings. She insisted that his family didn't like her, but Jay disagreed. Although it took them a while to warm up to newcomers, he had no doubt that they would get there. Erika's current behaviors were both embarrassing him and making her look bad.

Since the relationship with Erika was deteriorating, Jay saw being with his family as a welcoming release to the ever-present stress he felt at both home and work. As far as he was concerned, seeing his family a couple of times a week was not a big deal. This was an important cultural piece of him that he wasn't giving up, and he couldn't understand why this was a problem now. For years he had spent his off-hours this way, and Erika had never complained.

Jay couldn't help but feel incredibly resentful toward Erika. It seemed that having the baby totally changed her. She had become more critical; things that never bothered her before now seemed to be a huge sticking point. It bothered him that she had become so controlling of his time. Her questions had an underlying tone that set him off, turning instantly to anger. It had become such a hot button issue that every time she brought it up, he got upset and stormed off.

YOU ARE BOTH RIGHT

There may be a great deal of resentment and blame, piled sky high and standing in the way of improvement, as each party sees the other as culpable, and both don't know how to get past the mountain of bitterness that stands squarely between them.

Couples in this type of dynamic find themselves in their head a great deal. Since communicating with one another is largely ineffective, it is understandably avoided. But the hurt remains cycling as negative commentary in your head.

Both Jay and Erika, in the preceding scenario, feel validated about their feelings of anger and resentment, and as is the case with many couples' issues, both are right. There is no bad guy here; both parties have legitimate feelings about each other, and the choices they have made impact one another. Acting out on these feelings shows that one is angry or frustrated, but it fails to constructively get at the core of the issue.

Remember that having a reaction without appropriate communication robs you and your partner of the opportunity to get to a place of real resolution. The anger here is just a symptom. It is the way some convey a bigger need. In Erika and Jay's case, it may hide the underlying sadness, loneliness, or feelings of rejection and neglect. Because of the anger, it is hard to get to the real issue, which is a growing feeling of disconnect in the relationship.

All the emotions and anger are valid and common, as this couple adjusts to being married, becoming parents, and dealing with extended family. They have yet to learn how to work together and be a team, while still respecting each other.

In this situation, important needs of each party were not acknowledged, and it led to an escalation in defensiveness and anger on both sides. By not communicating correctly, they were both free to play off the assumptions and interpretations of their subjective perceptions. For Erika, this led her to think that Jay did not care about her or their child. While for Jay, the perception of this absolute change in Erika after the birth of their child had no room for him or his family.

Every time they tried to talk about it, the discussion would escalate within minutes. Before long they would be hurling their assumptions, misinterpretations, and worst fears across the room as verbal daggers. Realizing that they were treating one another like hated enemies, they came to us for help.

Working on putting aside anger, past hurts, and reactive shutdowns, they came up with some rules for when they should and should not communicate. The hard-and-fast rule was that when things escalated (that is, if either one of them got angry and raised their voice, or shut down and stopped engaging), the conversation would stop and be picked up at a later point. A supporting rule was that ending the discussion was to be respected by both parties as a boundary. That meant that they agreed to give one another space and not reengage until they were calm.

Communicating with guidelines was hard at first, and on several occasions, they slipped up and had to remind one another of the rules. This may have initially felt a little awkward, but it opened the door to deeper conversations that they had never had before. These discussions enlightened both of them and gave them an ability to see and understand each other more fully.

Expressing themselves without hostility and rage exposed a different set of feelings, which were more genuine. They pointed at the missing components in the relationship. Getting their needs met thus became easier.

SOLUTIONS AND STRATEGIES

Removing the Bad

Having arguments that escalate into explosive fights is a choice. It may not feel like much of a choice when you are in the heat of a battle, but understand that such a conflict sets you up for failure and creates a lose-lose scenario for both of you. You're given a choice. You can either continue down that same failing path or change matters for the better.

The truth is that conflict, arguments, and fights can simply be avoided. The common pitfalls and triggers that normally spark up and escalate a negative interaction can be averted, redirected, or defused by either one of you. Many fights are prompted by off-handed negative comments, body language, or other small gestures that can quickly escalate. So you can choose to calmly talk about them. That's why it is so imperative to use the previous chapters' strategies as a baseline from which you can build upon.

When you adopt a solution-based outlook, you can work together to identify the habits and triggers that lead you down the rabbit hole to the same unsatisfying results. Fighting and escalating will always fail to deliver change. Insist on not going there with each other.

Remember that cultivating the ability to communicate effectively and to listen and speak while staying calm and respectful is the only way to break down walls of resentments, defensiveness, and anger.

LAINEY & STEWART

Revisited

Lainey and Stewart were still walking on eggshells days after their fight (introduced in chapter 4). Stewart called our office to discuss the blowout, and he was able to reflect on their argument with fresh eyes. When he looked at it from a more rational perspective, he was able to admit that he may have overreacted. Lainey was not a spender. She was not fiscally irresponsible. It may be that she was not hearing him on cutting back, and that needed to be addressed, but it was unfair of him to attack her.

We encouraged Stewart to speak to Lainey about his feelings and stressed the importance of remaining calm throughout that discussion, so that instead of escalating, getting upset, and storming off, a real discussion could take place—one focused on devising an agreed-upon budget. Stewart agreed that he needed to talk to Lainey, instead of his usual habit of sitting around hoping that she would break the ice and apologize.

When he got off the phone, he felt better. He knew what to do.

That night, they had a serious discussion. He really tried to hold himself back and not react negatively to her words. Lainey noted his efforts and acknowledged that he was a lot less defensive, which made her want to continue talking. It was helpful to hear each other out without the shutdowns and brush-offs that usually occurred. The positive conversation and the successful result of cutting back and a surprisingly better managed household gave them the motivation to have more of these discussions in the future.

Moving Away from Blame

Unfortunately, it is all too easy to fault your partner, to pick at their shortcomings, and in the process fail to see your own role in the faltering relationship. The truth is that, in most situations, both parties are partially culpable. Usually there is no one person totally responsible for the negative place that you end up cycling in. Turning the communication in a positive direction can make this back and forth more productive.

Start with You

Taking ownership of who you are as an individual human being—strengths, weaknesses, flaws, and all—allows you to deal with the relationship issues without seeking to blame the other person. Pushing yourself to accept accountability for your actions, instead of shifting fault, reduces the reactivity and the defensiveness you both feel.

Respond Rather Than React

Instead of just reacting to one another as you always do, become aware of what is said and done in the moment. Clarify and correct in real time when the perceived hurt occurs. Do not store your hurts away. Learn to release them in a healthy way. Taking a different approach will nip issues in the bud and work in your favor by showing your partner your now positive intention.

Ask Instead of Indict

Understand that your thoughts and feelings are not facts, but mere interpretations of a moment in time. It could be that your interpretations are spot on, but in the same way, they could be completely off base. Checking in with your partner gives you the ability to calmly understand their thoughts and feelings without just assuming that theirs will negate yours.

JIM & STACY

Your Face Says It All

Jim stopped the couple's session to address Stacy's obvious nonverbal behavior, the frequent eye rolling, sighs, and incredulous looks that had accompanied every statement he made since they sat down. It was not a behavior that he was willing to continue to accept from his wife. Stacy agreed that she was a demonstrative person but disagreed with Jim's assessment that this happened "all the time."

They left our office with a plan: Every time that Stacy used one of these negative expressions, Jim was to calmly bring it to her attention and allow her the opportunity to catch it in the moment. He was also to mark the event to get a true reading of the frequency of these behaviors. After a few weeks, Stacy was surprised to see how many times Jim had to nudge her. It was significant enough for her to take note and have positive discussions with Jim on how to address the problem.

This willingness to work together on this issue was a huge turning point. It had a positive impact on Jim, allowing him to step into the supportive role we talked about with relish. He took it upon himself to help shepherd Stacy out of these moments, and they had great fun coming out of these potentially tense triggering events by being lighthearted and poking fun at the moment.

Just Stop Yourself

The verbal and nonverbal utterances that keep conflicts going must be addressed and eliminated. The eye rolling, sighs, and under-the-breath mumblings have the potential to blow up in your face. There are moments where just a doubtful look can end a positive discussion. Both parties must be aware of the unnecessary and triggering nonverbal responses they utilize. Some of these are simply habitual. It's just what you do when you disagree or take issue with their commentary, yet others are your way of letting your partner know your unhappiness and dissatisfaction within the moment. Regardless of the reasons behind these not-so-subtle ways of communicating, they work against you, sabotaging your marriage. If a person is open and minimally defensive, this behavior can definitely be changed.

End the name-calling and negative remarks, the withholding, blame shifting, and pity plays. None of these work and will only serve to increase the distress and toxicity in your home. Whenever they come up, allow each other the space to retract and apologize. If conflict continues to escalate as a result, use your code word and then, later, when it's calm, bring your concerns to the discussion table.

If these types of potentially inflammatory communication habits are common in your home, it may be time to put in stop measures that allow you to think before you speak. Choose a wiser course of action by picking your battles. Let insignificant matters go—don't allow them to sabotage your progress and derail the efforts of fixing your relationship's foundation.

WE SAY:

As most people know, telling your partner that they are out of control, or that they need to calm down, never works. Once you say that one person is out of control, then you are implying that the other is the one in control. Refrain from doing so.

REBUILDING THE GOOD

Again, Take Up Talk Time

The goal is to learn how to communicate effectively, but on the journey there you will need to improve on whatever passes for communication now. There are the poor habits that are already integrated into your responses and behaviors toward one another. There are triggers linked to anger and resentment, which can manifest as disrespect and disinterest. Because of these past behaviors, you must have a way of ensuring these discussions don't deteriorate or escalate.

The importance of using your code word/phrase to avoid falling into those same bad patterns cannot be overstated. You are already conditioned to go toward the negative, and there must be a tool in your arsenal to stop that progression. Having an apparatus that allows you to protect the relationship at any moment is absolutely crucial as it serves as your protective boundary. By agreeing to honor the immediate disengagement that a code word signifies, you both take on the role of gatekeeper.

You have been appointed as protectors of your marriage, and it is your responsibility to ring the alarm and not allow for further deterioration. If your goal is to fix your marriage and connection, you must commit to use of a code word, even if it seems silly and you don't see its value initially. This verbal indicator serves as a signal for both of you to *shut up and shut it down* for now, thus avoiding the damage that happens in real time when couples have no filter and, in a moment, can destroy months, even years of working on your marriage.

Coming together to talk after a timed break can help you move from circling around the problem to working on the solution. Applying this intervention becomes even more important when conflict has the potential to get explosive. When used appropriately, the code word or phrase provides safety from having a scary roller-coaster relationship, not only by stopping the descent to further conflict and hurt, but in it building hope by showing you both as committed to change.

This must be followed.

GEORGE & MARTHA

Code-Word Conundrum

George hated the code phrase. He felt it was juvenile and felt ridiculous saying, "I think we need more succulents," so instead of finding a more appropriate phrase, he just refused to say it. Doing so derailed their progress as every week he and Martha would show up for couples counseling after a new blowout fight or crisis. With George refusing to use the code word, they could not stop their reactionary behaviors from taking over. They treaded water for a while until George relented and then change happened rapidly.

For George and Marsha, taking a break and having a tool to halt the arguing was the one thing standing in their way to respectful dialogue. Once they were able to eliminate this obstacle, they got along wonderfully.

More on the Code Word

It is important to note that this code word/phrase has to be used properly to be effective. It should not be used to stifle your partner after you utter a vicious statement. Meaning that you can't get your say and then deny your partner a response via use of said code word. Using it this way will reinforce it as a negative tool. It also cannot be used to stop a difficult conversation that you just don't want to have and have no intention of continuing.

Then how, you may ask, is the code word to be used?

Good question. It is to be used to stop the progression into a negative interaction.

RITA & ANTON

Fight Avoided

Rita could read Anton's agitation in his body language, so she knew what was coming. She sensed that she was about to get an opportunity to use their therapist's funny code phrase. They had vicious fights and although she was skeptical that the code phrase would work, she was willing to try anything to avoid having one tonight.

When he snapped at her for forgetting to pick up milk, she said the agreed on phrase "Man, this Chinese food is salty." He looked like he was going to blow, and then he acknowledged, "You're right. I've had a tough day and it's not fair to take it out on you. I'm sorry." Rita was shocked. She couldn't believe how gracefully they avoided a fight.

This phrase is not just about calling out your partner. We all have to be aware, as you may be the one who is escalating the fight.

KEVIN & KARLA

Kindly Chill

Kevin was frantically typing to get the paperwork out to the client before midnight. He had missed two deadlines in the last month and knew one more was going to result in the dreaded "meeting" with upper management. Karla came into the room and softly put her arms around him as he typed. When she started talking about their social calendar, he could feel his anxiety increasing fast. Not only was he not getting his work done, he felt irritated that she was planning his weekends without consulting him.

Feeling this flood of emotion, Kevin knew he needed to calm down and identify what feelings were connected to what. He used their code slogan to keep the moment light and not let himself get to the moment where he would take out his mounting stress on Karla, because it wasn't fair to her.

Use of the word/phrase should play out like a bell in a boxing match—once uttered, it means an immediate time-out. And as soon as it's implemented, physically separate. Go to different rooms. Go outside. But make sure to leave each other's presence. People will often not want to adhere to this rule, intent to keep it going, but if used correctly, the code signal ensures that the original conversation will continue after a brief cool down.

Set a timer for a ten- or twenty-minute break to calm down, breathe deeply, and remember the original goal of the discussion. Focus on what was going on in the room at the time the code word/phrase was used.

- What happened?
- What was the trigger?
- What did *you* do wrong?
- Why did you get hurt/angry?

Give each other space to deescalate and then come back to the discussion table to resume the conversation, this time without anger or cattiness. But first, when you come back together, tell one another your perspective of what happened, with the goal being to understand what led it to deteriorate in the first place.

This is *not* a time to retool and argue down the hurtful statements that have already been made—just the opposite. Acknowledge your part in what went wrong, apologizing for anything hurtful or insensitive that *you* may have said in anger. Defensiveness won't serve you well. Recognize that all-or-nothing generalizations character assassinate your partner unfairly. Although your mate may have faults, getting their buy-in to improve upon those faults requires that you not minimize your partner. "I'd like you to do more of this" is very different from "You never do this." Practice working on the former.

Talk Time in Place of Conflict

Use talk time as an alternative framework to conflict. In this safe space you can ask for what you need rather than complain or critique your partner for not providing it. By highlighting areas where your partner is doing well and asking for ongoing improvement, you start to make headway.

Everyone wants to feel good and validated for what they contribute to the relationship. Making your partner feel valued or appreciated creates a better delivery system for the tough conversations that periodically need to be had. It allows the discussions to move from a problem-focused discussion to a solution-focused one, where instead of looking to blame each other for the problem, you put your two heads together seeking the solution.

Most of the available literature on conflict resolution promotes "I" statements when delivering requests, because it avoids the more blaming "you" statement. For example, "I am angry" doesn't have the same finger-pointing sting to it as "You make me so angry," allowing the other party to hear you better without it triggering defensiveness or a counterattack.

You both need solutions, something to hold onto that provides hope that tomorrow this issue will get better. Using talk time as an action-based venue that is constructive and optimistic allows you both to start believing that change is possible.

My Bad, I Am Sorry

Instead of the formerly ineffective back and forth, you can acknowledge your part in the dispute by simply saying sorry, taking ownership when you mess up, and being respectful of your partner at the same time.

This is not an "I'm sorry that you are mad" or an "I'm sorry that you took it that way"—doing so means that you are just apologizing for their invalid feelings. It is okay for your mate to have a reaction, even if it is one you didn't intend. You can still empathize and be apologetic without taking blame. More positive approaches include these:

- "I'm sorry. That came out wrong."
- "My intention was not to hurt you. I apologize if I did."
- "Let me take that back, babe. It was not what I meant."

Through these constructive discussions, a pattern will emerge that shows you both where you could do better. Start recognizing the behaviors you do that inflame the situation and work on eliminating those. Doing so can only help your relationship to grow and strengthen.

Being Authentic

Through admitting that you made a mistake, you are revealing your vulnerability to your partner. Conceding that you did something wrong, and taking an apologetic stance, eliminates issues that can otherwise fester.

We consistently meet couples who explode over the smallest, most insignificant issues. Many times, these are unnecessary reactions, where the punishment does not fit the crime. A simple apology in the moment and acceptance can resolve these smaller issues that act as a bridge to bigger issues. At the same time, it makes your spouse feel validated and strengthens your connection.

Also, adding a gesture to your verbal apology goes a long way. Take your partner's hand. Give a hug. Take a beat to look into his or her eyes as you deliver your apology. It will feel more heartfelt to the receiving party and sweetly smooth over a potentially explosive moment.

Acknowledging Progress

Knowing your mate is trying to work with you, rather than against you, will lead you to make allowances and accept their apology much quicker than you would otherwise. Doing so reinforces that the quality behavior will continue. Failing to acknowledge the apology makes the other feel as if there is no point to their attempts. Taking the approach of "he/she should have been doing this all along" robs you of an opportunity for a loving and kind moment. Take all of these that you can get. Hardening against your spouse when they are trying works against change. Couples need to be particularly mindful to not quash each other's efforts. Instead, you can say this:

- "Thanks for apologizing, it means a lot to me."
- "You have been doing a good job. I appreciate the efforts you've been making."

Fighting explosively not only doesn't work, it actually serves to weaken the relationship. In the next chapter, we will examine what happens when negative communication and conflict lead to the loss of your connection. Weakening your bond serves to derail closeness and well-being, sealing couples into Married Roommates status.

CHAPTER 5

KEY TAKEAWAYS

✔ Disagreeing and conflict in marriage is normal. Two parties must now make joint decisions, and they won't always agree or align on even the simplest issues.

✔ Lacking communication to resolve problems, poor habits of blaming, shaming, and attacking often lead couples to explosive fights and a subsequent feeling of walking on eggshells.

✔ Issues are left unresolved and the hurt remains, often acting as an accelerant in future disagreements, getting you so heated that you act in ways that sabotage and destroy your connection.

✔ This level of anger and hostility usually triggers the fight-or-flight response, sometimes without our awareness or control. In this state, we usually do the most damage to our relationship. When out-of-control people often say and do things that they later regret.

✔ The fights themselves can be brutal and leave people stuck in their heads and feelings, reeling from the pain. We rarely come back to fix the damage done in those moments, and it allows us to feed the negative commentary in our head about our mate.

✔ The lack of repair and fear around revisiting the conflict often makes it difficult for couples to move on and makes it challenging for couples to feel motivated in engaging one another on difficult subjects.

✔ Work on avoiding and eliminating explosive fights before they even begin. Do so by being aware of conversations in real time and pull them back if they escalate or start going into sensitive topics that will only blow up in your face. Those should be shelved for now, until you learn how to communicate effectively.

✔ Start with yourself and work on responding rather than reacting. Just stop yourself, and be aware of your nonverbal and verbal responses and triggers.

✔ Practice nipping potential problems in the bud before they form by offering a simple apology and taking responsibility where it is warranted. Validate and acknowledge each other's efforts toward change. Even a tiny little movement in the right direction should be celebrated.

✔ Code words can be the key to stopping the escalations that lead couples to fall off a cliff—use this technique as a protective boundary to avoid further damage. Be the protector and gatekeeper of your marriage. Come back to the discussion table and calmly clarify, explain, and ask by taking ownership and apologizing for your part in the negative interaction.

✔ Schedule time to talk and get past the defensiveness, anger, and resentment that have stopped real authentic talk in the past. Use talk time to ask for what you need and learn to be more open to hearing what your partner needs from you.

DISAPPEARING CONNECTIONS

Suffering in Silence

After ten years together, Rob never could have imagined that his life would culminate in this moment. For years, the writing was on the wall, but he always assumed so much of the hardships, the disconnect, the lack of sex, and the criticisms were all a part of marriage.

He sat in the bathroom taking deep breaths. He could always rely on that safe space to escape being in the same space as Sophia. He could do everything right, but of course there would always be something that fell through the cracks; it was inevitable. What was also inevitable was that of all his successes, Sophia could only see his failures.

These days he was conditioned to hold his tongue, knowing that any utterance would bring on a huge fight. It never went well, so he just avoided talking, worried about the toxic and hurtful things he might say. Sometimes it just seemed easier to let her unleash on him—spit it out and cool off—than to have her take weeks to recover from the hurtful comments that he might say to her out of anger. He knew that firsthand.

He was sleeping in the living room again, after getting an infraction for checking his phone during dinner. Sophia was off stewing in the bedroom. He racked his brain thinking of all of her hypocrisy. For the last four nights she had taken calls or researched on her phone during dinner. He knew they had an agreement, but it was more her agreement anyway. He didn't see the big deal about a phone at the dinner table the way she did. She broke it, and he followed. In some way he had hoped the rule was "over." The consequence tonight showed it wasn't.

They had agreed to reduce eating out to control their credit card debt, which was also her idea. In similar fashion it became okay for her to go out with friends, but the scrutiny of any spending on his end became catastrophic. The same could be said for parenting interventions, boundaries with in-laws, or anything else. It seemed his wife always had the books and the online research from experts to back up the new limitations, exceptions, or structures that would be implemented into his life, but rarely did she model it into her own. He wanted to fight back, but it always came out wrong. The arguments left him constantly feeling resentment.

Then today, he finally exploded. He didn't know what came over him when he told her he was done, that he wanted out of their marriage. It was true—the loneliness, lack of appreciation, and void of emotional connection between them finally caused something in him to snap.

THE ROAD TO ROOMMATES

The connection between a couple is hard to define. At its core is the bond, the chemistry, the essence, or synergy that exists between two people, which can manifest as anything from playfulness and fun to empathy and tenderness. It is the closeness, the magic, and certain *je ne sais quoi* that you share. This connection fuels your love for that other person. It's the reason your eyes light up when she walks into the room, why you daydream about each other and spend so much time together. It's why you ask if he had anything to eat that day, and why you laugh at his jokes. It's also why you run home to tell her the good or bad news first, before all others, and why you insist that it is not right to go to bed mad. There's a reason you ended up together in the first place.

Unfortunately, couples let these moments of closeness fade, and over time, they start to take their connection for granted. Despite it being the relationship's bloodline, the connection is easily ignored and pushed out of the spotlight when the day-to-day priorities take over the emotional partnership.

You may not even notice at first, but before you know it, a long time has passed since you spent any alone time, laughed together, or caught each other's eyes across the room.

The foundation of this kind of bond rests on mutual feelings of trust, respect, empathy, reciprocity, and deep attachment. When these qualities are aligned, the core bond between the two of you is one of a deep connection. When letdowns and disappointments regularly taint these qualities, the bond between a couple becomes disconnected and untethered.

For many couples, once the closeness fully disappears, it takes the connection with it and you are left feeling as if you are not in love anymore.

The good news is that this situation is reversible, and so much can be adjusted to correct this course. It might not exactly produce the same butterflies you had at the onset, but it can be just as good. The heart-fluttering spark you once had for each other can be claimed once again, but this time you have to do the work to get it.

PRIORITIZE EACH OTHER

Relationships will naturally go through phases of highs and lows in terms of connection and intimacy. Whether you have more high times than low depends on your behavior toward one another and the regard you give the relationship. The day-to-day level of consideration and interest that you give each other fosters either positive or negative feelings. Once negative thoughts take root—although you continue performing your functional duties in parallel—you stop treating your relationship as something important and fail to see its real value.

You may even be unaware that you prioritize the logistics of your life together ahead of each other. It is usually not an intentional move, but the consequences remain the same. Your emotional connection becomes an afterthought, neglected and often buried under mountains of routines and resentments from the shared life.

It takes time to get to the place where your relationship morphs completely into roommates. This deterioration of a couple's connection is composed of countless little moments of disappointment, hurt, and not showing up for one another.

These are the moments when you feel alone, misunderstood, or unappreciated. They are day-to-day, inconsequential, small letdowns in reliability and trust, like him habitually eating dinner on his own, not checking in with her, even though he knows that it makes her upset. Or she's continuously disrespecting his family, although she knows it hurts his feelings. The more of these moments that pile up, the more disconnected you feel, and the more you grow apart from one another. This behavior builds a wall between you, which eventually ends up severing the emotional connection.

When communication is not effective at correcting these negative patterns, resentments accumulate at a more rapid pace and build that barrier between you at double time. You both contribute to that wall by not being present, by barely noticing each other or interacting in any genuinely connected way. You sleep back-to-back in bed, physically present but emotionally checked out. Conversations become the exchange of simple pleasantries, sometimes even feeling forced and awkward. You stop sharing your innermost thoughts, joys, and sorrows with each other. You don't trust each other with these private and personal thoughts anymore. Your vulnerability is no longer accessible.

With nothing to feed your emotional connection, the sustenance disappears, and eventually you stop talking, sharing, and asking for one another's opinion or advice. You usually don't do it with spite; you naturally gravitate to other outlets rather than each other. You may still be in the same room but choose to pay more attention to your devices than each other.

On the surface, nothing seems wrong. You rationalize zoning out on your phone, falling into rabbit holes of "worthy" news items, social media updates, and a day's worth of emails and texts. The truth is these time fillers distract you from the scarcity of conversation, from each other, and from the reality of an unspectacular life together.

Past mistakes of hurting each other and leaving wounds unresolved have unfortunate consequences in the present. It cements a reality where two parties are emotionally withdrawn, no longer showing up or trusting the other with their authentic selves. You retreat inward, showing each other the same facade that you give the rest of the world. Hiding behind the projected facade just feels safer. So much so that you don't even remember what it feels like to genuinely connect with one another.

You go through the motions every day, unable to locate the "on" switch for that spark of meaningfulness with one another. You accept the facade as real, too let down and spent to care.

Your vulnerability is hidden under lock and key. Heart-to-heart conversations are something you used to do. Answers now look like "fine" and "good" instead of the colorful descriptions they used to be.

BENNY & KEISHA

Missed Connections

Benny's phone vibrated in his pocket. He knew what the text would say before he even opened it. Although he hoped he was wrong this time, there it was on his phone—Keisha canceling on him yet again because of some minor detail with the kids. He was beyond disappointed. Waves of anger, resentment, and bitterness washed over him as he fought to rein in his emotions. Benny loved his kids, but these were not emergencies, and this type of helicoptering seemed to happen all too often. After all the fights and talks about trusting her, Keisha had canceled on him again. He couldn't believe that because his eldest had a book report due in three days, Keisha had prioritized a trip to the library over meeting him for coffee.

He had been looking forward to tonight. He thought that he finally got through to her about the importance of them having nights out without the kids. It infuriated Benny to think that Keisha was just hearing him out, with no intention of setting this time aside for them. He tried not to be narrow-minded, not to be the cliché of the father jealous of his wife's attention toward the kids, but he found it increasingly difficult to control the sadness that washed over him at the loss of the connection with Keisha.

TRUST IN SHORT SUPPLY

Despite the lack of interest, it is the missing element of trust that ultimately keeps you away from your partner. People immediately think of trust in terms of fidelity, but trust is so much bigger than that. At face value, Benny and Keisha's situation doesn't appear to be related to trust, since he got upset, mad, even sad. However, at the root of his feelings toward Keisha, deep disappointment registers as a consistent letdown, resulting in an inability to count on and believe in her. That boils down to trust.

Trust violations abound when you let one another down by not doing what you say you will, or by not having each other's back and doing things that consistently highlight your own self-interest.

Letting each other down in countless ways has eaten up your faith in one another. The inconsistencies in reliability do damage to our ability to trust. This is usually done unintentionally by failing to prioritize one another and by creating a situation where the playing field is consistently uneven, where one party has more to carry than the other. It is even further reinforced by missing words of encouragement and praise.

When the formality of acknowledgment disappears, and the niceties end, it takes along with it your patience, softness, and positive regard. You simply stop believing in each other. You even stop liking each other.

In this state, you are less likely to put your heart and openness on the line again. You fortify yourself against each other and live a surface life together, devoid of meaningful interactions. Without a serious fix, your regard for one another just continues to unravel, getting to a point where even kindness and compassion disappear, along with the empathy and care you once felt for each other.

When you don't receive empathy from your partner, and you feel you give and give but don't feel appreciated, eventually you have the unfortunate realization that the one person who will take care of you is *you*. Subsequently, you detach yourself for your own preservation. You just escape. Maybe you binge-watch Netflix on your own, fixate on a new hobby, volunteer, or increase your time with friends.

No longer reliant on your union, your marriage, for acceptance, love, or even friendship, you find something that makes you feel better, whether it be a new gym or a new friend. He does the poker night or action films with his boys. She does after-work drinks with her friends.

Unnourished, both parties get to a place where they don't have the strength, time, or energy to nurture one another. There is no ill will in the intention. It's just a reality that is created by failing to nourish each other, which leaves you both running on empty as Married Roommates.

JOHN & LESLIE

Bridgeable Differences

John loved anything sports-related, which kept him in great shape. By 5:00 a.m., he was on his morning run, today being no exception. Although he felt exhausted, physically and mentally, he needed this time to clear his head. He liked being outside, and he often organized trips to the surrounding ocean, lakes, and forests. Hiking and camping had always been a big part of his life. He refused to let the demands of their busy lives change this basic love of nature.

Meanwhile, Leslie grew increasingly resentful of his "me time," calling him selfish and self-absorbed. She didn't understand that these activities kept his depression and despair at bay. Life with three young kids was hard—harder than he would have ever imagined, and he didn't want to be an unhappy partner and father, like his wife. Not only did she become a nag, but she became boring and old to a point where it impacted his attraction to her. It's like she just became a middle-aged mom overnight, losing her sense of being a fun, vibrant woman.

◾

These days, Leslie liked to stay at home, but early in their relationship, she had joined John on all his nature excursions. Eventually that stopped and they developed different hobbies, no longer having much in common. John would hint at bike riding, rafting, sailing, diving, skiing, or just hiking, but she didn't enjoy spending time with him anymore. He would just lecture her about healthy living and what she needed to do to get her life in order. She learned that if she expressed muted interest but never came through with planning or attending, it ended uncomfortable moments and avoided a fight.

They got by living totally separate lives, ignoring each other
and living for the kids. Lately they couldn't even be in the same
room without being disrespectful or even borderline rude with
one another.

UNMET EXPECTATIONS
AND UNFULFILLED NEEDS

While most people don't go into relationships focusing on the negative, failing to get your needs met over time changes you. Succumbing to the unhappiness you feel, you become unwilling to reciprocate what you yourself have not received in terms of empathy and understanding. You refuse to give and to compromise, and, as a result, you fall into patterns of living separate, disjointed lives under the same roof.

This divide usually isn't one person's fault. Rather, it is the system, routines, and habits that you put into place that become the actual culprit.

WHEN MINDSET SHIFTS TO THE NEGATIVE

One of the biggest factors that facilitates the progression into Married Roommates is your own mindset or, more precisely, your internal dialogue. If the way you view your mate turns negative, your dissatisfaction grows. You stop being kind and complimentary. You stop giving them the benefit of the doubt and tend to assume the worst.

This poisonous negativity leads you to start noticing more and more habits that you dislike and disapprove of with regard to your partner. These become magnified in your head, and before you know it, they muscle out all positive thoughts. The optimistic, internal narrative you once had completely turns negative, and, as a result, so does your behavior toward one another. Not only are you not as thoughtful or interested in each other as before, but almost the opposite is true. You are bored by his stories and find fault in the very same traits you used to love about him. You are annoyed by her incessant nagging and find it unappealing and needy.

One partner may be the originator of this mental decline, but it soon infects both parties. When one person has nothing to give to water the other, eventually you both turn off.

Failing to connect emotionally, at best, will rob you of your intimacy and connection. At their worst, couples become disrespectful and contemptuous of one another. When nothing changes over time, communication often continues to deteriorate, leading to dissatisfaction, sadness, and frustration. One or both parties harbor resentment and negative feelings, which increases anger, disappointment, and disillusionment. Without any fix, eventually you arrive at total disconnect, apathy, and passivity. At that point, couples disengage and pull away. You simply give up. It can get to the point that the structure of your lives will be the only thing holding you together.

ELAINE & JOSHUA

Like Ships in the Night

Elaine was in the living room watching an old episode of Seinfeld when Joshua walked in more than an hour late. She thought about asking where he had been but ultimately decided that it wasn't worth a fight. It surprised her that she didn't really care.

*Joshua saw Elaine sitting there in the dark and groaned
internally. Great, she was probably waiting for him so she could
interrogate him about his day. To his surprise, there was no
response to his mumbled greeting. He sighed his relief quietly
and continued silently to the den, where he spent most evenings.*

COMPOUNDING THE CRACK

As things go off the rails in your relationship, the situation unfortunately starts to affect the physical, emotional, economic, and
social parts of your lives. You may not sleep well or eat right, and
you make choices that disrupt things even further, like stopping
the morning run, avoiding get-togethers with friends, or canceling
the gym membership, which creates a space that additional bad
habits rush to fill, creating an even less desirable new normal.

SARAH & DAMON

Disconnected Daily

*Sarah thought about her day and tried to control the anxiety she
felt as she looked at the long to-do list in her hand. She was a
stay-at-home mom, so everything that had to do with the children
or the home was her sole responsibility. Although Damon was a
good father and provided well for them as the breadwinner, she
felt as if he minimized her contributions to the household. He did
not understand the amount of work she did on a daily basis and
often made comments about her so-called easy life.*

It wasn't always this way. In the early years of their marriage, both of them were appreciative and affectionate. Damon used to be in awe of her parenting skills and made her feel so valued that she didn't mind falling into the traditionalist household he envisioned. She figured that she would go back to work after her first child, Connor, was born, but between her worry about leaving Connor with a babysitter and Damon's insistence that Connor needed her home, she relented and so had passed ten years. Their kids were older now and needed her less and less as time went on. Nowadays, she thought more and more about going back to work, but every time she brought it up to Damon, he shot it down, always evoking her guilt by saying that the kids still needed her at home.

It seemed that through the years, he had become more critical and less understanding. If he came home early and found her watching TV while folding the laundry, he would make a cutting comment. If she was on the computer trying to set up playdates for the kids, he would assume that she was on Facebook gossiping with friends. He never thanked her or asked about her day. Instead, he made snarky comments to family and friends about her charmed life and how he carried the entire household by himself.

As his put-downs continued, Sarah started to distance herself, both in the bedroom and out of it. It was the reason behind many of the fights they had been having lately. As usual, he could not see her point of view, and talking about it led them nowhere. If anything, it even made things worse. When she finally opened up and told him how she felt, he found a way of twisting her words around, making himself sound like the injured party.

Damon worried about work. He felt as if his superiors were not happy with his performance. No one said anything directly, but he had a nagging feeling that they felt he wasn't putting in the time like everyone else. He was one of a handful of fathers at the office, in a young company, mostly composed of ambitious millennials who never complained about being at work sixty, even seventy, hours a week. He realized that their enthusiasm for the job made him look bad. At some point, clocking out at 6:00 p.m. now seemed like leaving early. Damon tried to leave work around then to have some time with the kids, but he figured that since his job was the family's only source of income, he would have to stay at work later and spend the weekends with his kids.

Sarah was usually furious when he got home later than she expected. She seemed to not understand or care that he was competing with the time management skills of twenty-year-olds and that his job could be on the line. Damon did not understand what her problem was. This was their agreement from the onset of their marriage. Now she acted like she couldn't handle the kids by herself in the evenings. His staying late created tension at home, but it was outside of his control as work seemed to get more and more demanding. Soon work had him going to the office every Saturday, just to keep up. He was stressed out, on edge with everyone and everything in his life, and lately his heartburn had him popping Tums every twenty minutes.

His thoughts often turned to his wife and the lack of empathy she seemed to have for the fear he felt. Instead of supporting him during this awful time, she was always on him, nagging him to be home early to spend more time with the kids, as if this was a choice. It was easy for her to cancel out the demands of his job, as she didn't feel the daily pressure of providing for the family and keeping them afloat. Her expectations were unrealistic. No matter how many times he explained that, she still didn't get it.

He felt so angry at her that lately all it took was a look or a sigh from her to get his blood boiling. Damon felt old, worn out, and bitter. He felt as if he were in a pressure cooker, and things were going to explode. He felt as if he was drowning in hopelessness and loneliness.

Sadly, she was right about one thing: lately he did not want to spend time with her. He avoided her, either focusing his energy on the kids or spending the evening in the garage, only coming back inside when it was time for bed. They hadn't had sex for months and for the first time in his life, he didn't really care. She must not care either, as she never initiated or made him feel as if it was important to her. He couldn't remember the last time they went out or had a good time with one another.

OKAY, NOW WHAT?

Without any meaningful improvements, years of living as room-mates and feeling unfulfilled take their toll. You have learned to ignore, punish, and condemn each other, isolating and disengaging yourselves emotionally. You have become emotional strangers. The layers of anger, resentment, and hurt have formed a seemingly immovable barrier to forgiveness and starting over.

The foundation to the barrier is the bad habits that govern your day-to-day behavior toward one another. They consistently feed the negative thoughts you have about each other, allowing you to create your own islands of reality, with the shared life in the center.

While you feel disconnected, unseen, and unheard by one another, life does go on.

It paints a bleak picture of the decades ahead—one that doesn't satisfy your daily existence. The connection feels muted and lacking, and inherently you understand that you need more to be fulfilled. Whether you act on that in a healthy way or an additionally damaging one remains to be seen.

It is our recommendation that you facilitate the change toward being good together, rather than just accept it and have the decision be taken away from you down the road, when the fix becomes less and less of a reality and people are left no options but to plan for a life apart.

IT IS NEVER TOO LATE

Your bond is like a living being that must be tended to and nourished regularly. And it must happen outside of the shared life, as it is not interchangeable with one of the many other hats you share with each other, so fixing the toaster or taking the kids to school doesn't earn you points in the marriage department.

When couples have lost the hope that their relationship can improve, they give up. They find themselves in this unfulfilling, empty, and lonely state of marriage, not because they are necessarily mismatched, incompatible, or individually problematic but because most do not have the tools to make a marriage successful.

Because they are missing these critical tools for success, and are largely unaware of it, both parties get to a point where they can only see their own unhappiness and misery. They cannot see how they both contributed to getting here, and that they are both hurt and disappointed with their life together.

Although you may fail to see hope, it is never too late. While turning it around is not easy, it is very possible.

If you want your home life to be easier and more harmonious, it is valuable to strive toward solutions instead of cycling around the problem. If you prefer to have your kids grow up witnessing a happy and stable home life, put in the time to fix your marriage. If you love your partner and want a better, closer relationship, it is worth the challenge of doing the work.

Turning your relationship around may require more intentional commitment and effort, but we believe that all Married Roommates can learn the tools to improve their life and feelings toward each other. Start by intentionally committing to doing what it takes and prioritize your marriage to somewhere near the top of your list, if not the very top.

SOLUTIONS AND STRATEGIES

Removing the Bad: The Power of Commitment

Instead of doing the same thing and expecting different results, you will need to do things differently. This requires a high level of commitment. You both have to try *and* continue trying every single day. You used to have this built-in devotion to one another that fueled your motivation to try. Unfortunately, that dedication came to a halt, not because you didn't love your mate, but because you rationalized the importance of working on your connection, convincing yourself that your relationship could handle anything.

Date nights stopped because the babysitter was too expensive, or because you had to work late at the office and the laundry still needed to get done. Spending quality time together became non-existent, because everything else was more important. People aren't always aware of what they prioritize, so be honest with yourself about what you choose to give your time and attention to.

> **WE SAY:**
>
> Take a moment to make a list of your biggest time expenditures—and be honest. Take it a step further and actually track your time over a day or a week. Outside of working and sleeping, are you spending most of your free time with your family, playing games, or watching TV, or are you on your phone tracking your fantasy team, answering emails, or putting together a work presentation? Are you content with how much of your life you allocate to actually living?

Once you recognize that nowadays the time you do spend with one another has become primarily an exchange of information, consisting of the day-to-day micromanagement that it takes to run your lives together, you can devote yourself to turning that around.

Acknowledging the real problem is half the journey, for you cannot fix what you do not recognize as problematic. All you can do is facilitate your part of the solution, change you, and let your mate work on improving their piece of the puzzle. Commit to changing your thoughts and behaviors instead of pointing fingers at your mate in hopes that they will change instead.

Maintain Your Marriage

Think about your body, house, and car. All of these elements of your life get serviced in ways that are preventive. You clean your gutters and get an oil change to avoid what may happen when you don't. You schedule physicals with your doctor to check in on your body. So much of what you do has a preventive lens. The state of your marriage should definitely be on the list of items tended to as well.

Move Focus from Bad to Good

Married Roommates have fallen into the habit of hyperfocusing on the bad and ignoring the good. It is a mindless and poisonous habit that must be manually reconfigured.

Rebuilding the Good: Make Your Marriage a Priority

When couples reflect back to earlier and simpler times when the relationship was going well, they forget how selfless they once were. How natural it was back then to go out of their way for one another, to do nice things, to listen and be helpful; in turn, they also received the same level of interest and attentiveness from their partner. That, in essence, is part of the solution.

The routine mundaneness of life can distract you from having deeper conversations. It can get to a place where you have nothing to say to one another unless it is about day-to-day reality or logistics. You shuffle through your tasks and responsibilities in parallel fashion, divide and conquer, showing up for each other in the most basic of ways. Life feels empty this way, devoid of the colors and magic that your relationship once had. It leads couples to exist in an uninspiring place, where you can't fortify or energize one another. Consequently, you become more tired and unhappy, just going through the motions alongside one another.

Work to regain that same level of priority and regard that you had in the beginning. The interest and attentiveness you had for each other at the onset occurred organically and just flowed. Now it has to be more thought out and intentional. Don't worry if you don't feel like doing it; do it anyway, trusting that the power of taking action intentionally will get you there.

Many of our clients walk in at the start of therapy and drop a disclaimer that they are hanging by a thread and basically hate each other. We tell them that it is totally fine, and from our perspective, it is to be expected. As long as you still show up and do the work, the feelings you currently feel toward your spouse should not be a deterrent. If you push through your resistance and just implement the strategies, day by day those feelings will start to change in the right direction. You can help the process along by being thoughtful and going out of your way for one another. Make your partner a cup of coffee in the morning, get their car washed, or grab that bagel they love from that deli down the road. Get creative on conveying the message that you want this to succeed.

Be Intentional

Being intentional is a different approach than hoping for autocorrection. It means doing something to ensure you get the results you want. You may not realize what you are currently prioritizing, whether by necessity or choice. Once you understand where the bulk of your attention goes, figure out what you can shift around to give your marriage a more significant piece of the priority pie. Become aware of the intentional behaviors and choices that actually improve harmony with your mate. Do more of them.

Rebuild Trust

Rebuilding trust takes time. Entangling and reconnecting the now loose fibers of believing in one another is a process. As previously discussed, getting hurt leads you to recede and erect a protective barrier around your feelings and vulnerability.

You must get back to the point where you allow each other a small entryway to rebuild trust. This requires reliability and follow-through on doing what you said you would, and the ability to garnish compassion for each other, where you take care of each other's feelings, even if you don't understand or don't agree. You can still be empathetic to another's feelings or needs if they differ from yours. Here are a couple of suggestions to help start the process:

- "Even though I don't necessarily agree, I know this upsets you and I feel for you. What can I do to make it better?"

- "It is hard for me to understand your feelings, but that doesn't matter. What matters is you, and I am here for you."

Make Reliability a Goal

Find three ways that you can be a better mate to your spouse. Think back to times that they have expressed being let down by you and endeavor to take these on once again—this time with intent and gusto. If your wife repeatedly asked you to clean the garage, email the receipts to the accountant, or organize the shed, all those tasks you have procrastinated on, surprise her by getting it done without being asked. Conversely, if your husband has repeatedly asked you to create a budget, make more room for him in the closet, or ask that you not post your day-to-day activities on social media, enter-tain him, even if you think that his request is ridiculous. In doing so, you get a much happier and more appreciative spouse, and in the process your home becomes a more joyful place. Sometimes all it takes is these little, thoughtful gestures to swing momentum in the right direction.

Elevate whatever you have decided to focus on to be a priority in your life. If your mate questions your eating habits, immerse yourself in ways that you could improve them. Buy cookbooks, download podcasts, hire a nutritionist. Ask your partner to join you in building a new healthy menu and go grocery shopping together.

If your partner makes comments about how you manage your financials, instead of being hurt and defensive, make it a point to turn this around. Take a class or read a book about financial management. Ask your spouse to sit with you and help you under-stand your monetary reality. Create financial goals and reward yourself when you achieve them. Make your partner aware that it matters to you to be a good team member and that your new-found interest in finances is because you care about their feelings and want to please.

JENNA & TODD

Putting on a Happy Face

Jenna was so relieved to see Todd's text, letting her know that he was grabbing dinner on his way home. She smiled to herself as she noted that since their talk last week, he was trying to be better at home by helping out and taking many errands off her plate. When she walked in the door an hour later and saw the lone

Costco chicken on the counter, she held herself back from making a snarky remark about the sad dinner he put together. Jenna took a deep breath and talked herself off the ledge, reminding herself that he tried and that they all loved Costco chicken anyway. She pasted a smile on her face, greeted him warmly, and pulled a salad from the refrigerator before setting the table.

Todd noticed Jenna standing there and followed her line of vision to the chicken. He knew his wife and was waiting for some comment about the nutritional value of the meal, blah, blah, blah. He waited for it, but she sucked it up and smiled. He was blown away that she actually caught herself before getting critical. He grabbed her in a bear hug so she wouldn't see his eyes glistening. He was so worried that their marriage had entered a death spiral, but this gave him confidence that she didn't want to give up on them.

Todd decided that he would go to the annual nurses ball with her; he knew how much it meant to her and he wanted to make her happy. He made a mental note to surprise her by getting his suit cleaned.

Find the Positivity

Practice noticing and commenting on the good. Try to do it in a *nongeneric way*, because showing authenticity and enthusiasm goes a long way. Don't just say, "You look nice." Instead, take notice and say, "Wow, babe. That's a nice color. You look incredible." Complimenting one another authentically will go a long way toward creating necessary change and a strengthened connection.

Cultivate increased kindness and caring. Do things for your mate *just because*, like picking up something that would make them happy on the way home. Do the thoughtful little extras that you used to do. All this requires is generosity of spirit, so remind your-self that you love this person and want to help them be happy and enjoy life. Doing so will generate the same level of care and concern back to you. If needed, have an external reminder system—put it on your calendar, leave yourself notes, set reminders, tell friends to check in with you. Do whatever will help to make sure you build this new habit, to avoid falling back into the status quo a week or two later when it is no longer top of mind.

Manually change your mindset from negative to positive by focusing on all your partner's strengths rather than on their weak-nesses. Work on changing the tape playing in your mind from all their deficiencies to all their strengths. Giving your partner appre-ciation and validation will usually be reciprocated. Remember to use that list of all their positive attributes and get into the habit of reminding yourself and your partner of all the good you bring to each other's lives.

In our practice we encourage couples to shift to a more strengths-based positive reinforcement system. Catch each other being good, rather than bad. Hold yourself back from comment-ing negatively, even if you notice slipups and fails. The move from negative to positive commentary will pay off, as intentionally high-lighting what you appreciate and value will create a more trusting environment that can withstand the difficult conversations that will regularly need to take place.

Make Time for Your Connection

Mindless distractions are everywhere, robbing you of your most precious commodity—time. You happily sign up for this thievery to take place, giving away your valuable time to an hour of televi-sion, social media, or mindless internet surfing. Since time cannot be manufactured or regenerated, once it's gone, it's truly gone, and you are left with the results of the time spent. Ironically, lack of time is a primary reason couples cite for not being more connected.

The reality is that you have to make this happen rather than expecting it to occur on its own. You both must take the initiative despite whatever else is going on. Being busy is a given. No one really has time. You need to engineer these moments through priority and intention by scheduling time together every week, blocking it off on your calendar, and committing to this time on a regular basis.

It is simple to get into the habit of spending time together intentionally. This may feel awkward at first, but if you can push through that initial discomfort, you will find a new depth to the relationship.

Spending time together does not have to be a big production, but it must be intentional. Good times can be had with some planning and even limited funds, whether inside at home or while out. The most important point is that you focus on activities where you can engage with one another and have fun. By planning ahead and not leaving things to the last minute, couples can always have something to look forward to.

The strategy may sound simple, but many of us don't do it consistently. And remember quality time is different than just time spent in the same physical space. Quality time refers to enjoyable moments spent together to have a good time, laugh, reconnect, and replenish the connection.

Give and Take Individual Me Time

Your partner and relationship cannot be the sole source of happiness and contentment. You both must take and give each other time to just be yourselves. This requires that you create a system where it is okay and even necessary to allow yourself and one another the time and space to self-care and do what makes you happy. That may mean just having alone time, going to the gym, hanging out with friends, or spending time on hobbies. Do not let guilt or negative feelings rob you of this time to replenish yourself. It is critical to sustainability and ongoing happiness.

Take Up Talk Time

Use this ongoing communication to rebuild the good. Take turns to identify a good and productive habit that you each wish to create in your day-to-day life. Discuss what you can both do to make this habit a reality. These activities should be focused on building your connection. Remember that it is consistency and repetitiveness of new behaviors that help create a new normal.

Instead of focusing on what you are missing and what your partner does wrong, target the behaviors that you want to see instead. Make these discussions positive, as doing so will still work to combat the triggers, poor habits, and core issues that are responsible for the disconnect and discord.

Talking Jar

Bring out the jar (as explained earlier) to drop in ideas for stimulating new conversations. These could be suggestions on new topics to discuss or tackle. These could be agenda items for ideas about trying new skills or activities or going to new places. While not every suggestion will be golden, try to keep an open mind when something new gets suggested, as it is valuable to, at times, just go along and see how things materialize. Not resisting and, even further, taking one for the team when necessary can lead to special, intimate moments that neither of you could have predicted.

Again, what's important here is just spending time together to reconnect. There is, however, value in trying things together that you have never done before. It is a shared adventure, and regardless of the outcome, you will be better off than just moving within predictable comfort zones.

Ask for Advice Once Again

Even if you sometimes don't totally agree with your partner's solicited opinions, appreciate that they care enough about you to offer their help. Value their effort and intent more than the content of the suggestion. Validate the fact that your partner tried to support you. It's as simple as stating, "Thanks for caring for me. It means a lot to have your input" or "I understand your point."

> ## WE SAY:
>
> Talk time and quality times are intentionally different. Talk time is used to heal and build communication and understanding for one another. Quality time is for the regaining of intimacy, fun, and likability.

Quality Time (QT) or Date Night

We often underestimate how much a weekly date can contribute to maintaining the connection and passion in a relationship. Dates can create the time and place for reconnecting. It can be time spent in the house or out, because both venues are ultimately important for your growing sense of intimacy. Again, having new experiences together will strengthen your connection and create something to look forward to.

Some call it "date night" or "quality time," but whatever you call it, carve out a time to encourage that more intimate and romantic connection between the two of you. It should become a consistent habit, something that you do regularly despite how busy and overwhelmed you find yourselves. So figure out what logistics you need to maneuver to make quality time a weekly or biweekly event, being realistic regarding what you can follow through on.

It doesn't matter really what you do during date night: Put on music at home, have fun and let loose. Have game nights and competitions, like cook-offs or dance-offs. Be intentionally less serious than you have been in the past. Start to let one another see the part that holds your playfulness and more carefree, fun qualities. Try a new activity and have a spontaneous moment together. Try a walk in nature, art exhibit, or a comedy improv show. It doesn't even have to be costly. This is where creativity and playfulness can kick in. Find shared activities that both parties can enjoy and get it on the books.

Out-and-About Ideas
- Take a class together (such as dancing, art, pottery, golf, paddle boarding). The list is endless.
- Explore local events. Most cities offer a wide array of yearlong activities (cultural fairs, festivals, museums, concerts, galleries). Get to know what fun activities and social events are going on near you.
- Use sites like Groupon, Living Social, and Goldstar to generate ideas.
- Go to an amusement park.
- Go hiking and bring a picnic.

- Try a live music venue.

- Go to a comedy show or a sporting event.

While-at-Home Ideas

- Cook a meal or a dessert together.

- Play a board game or any other games—anything from charades to truth or dare can be a fun way to shake up the status quo.

- Put on music, light some candles, and have a romantic night together.

- Get a karaoke machine and/or serenade each other.

Whether your date night is out and about or at home, find ways to be lighthearted, joke, banter, and be silly with one another. Refresh your flirting abilities and courting skills. Pretend you are on a first date or that you don't know each other as you do these new activities together to add a layer of playfulness.

One helpful strategy is to share the responsibility in planning these date nights. This is all intended to move you away from the stale dinner or movie and introduce fun, new options for your entertainment and bonding repertoire.

In the next chapter we will look at sex between Married Roommates, examining the relationship between a couple's sexuality and connection. Sex is an important component of a happy and fulfilled life together. Its slowdown and subsequent disappearance is another accelerant into roommate territory.

CHAPTER 6

KEY TAKEAWAYS

✔ The connection between two people is like a living being that must be cared for and worked on.

✔ How you behave toward one another and the regard you give the relationship sets the tone for its success. Consideration, interest, validation, appreciation, and caring—all will net you the relationship you want.

✔ Small, inconsequential daily letdowns have pulled you away from one another. You have built habits, systems, and routines that work against your connection. They fuel negative thoughts about your partner, allowing resentments to take root.

✔ A negative mindset will often lead you to expect negative outcomes and ultimately became a self-fulfilling prophecy. Negativity within the relationship is contagious, leading to a life marked by counterproductivity, mistrust, and resentment.

✔ Work against stagnation and negativity by intentionally prioritizing your relationship, giving time and focus to make sure you are providing the sustenance it needs.

✔ Push through your own resistance and show up to do the work, even if you don't feel like it or are skeptical that change can happen. Just by consistently using the strategies, your connection will evolve. Help it along by trying and by going out of your way to be reliable, thoughtful, and interested in one another.

- Rebuilding the good means focusing on the good. Practice finding the positive and commenting on it. Be intentional, and the results will come in faster than you could've imagined.

- Use talk time strategies to talk about replacing your poor habits with ones that will create better results.

- Take the initiative to make time for your connection. Remember, quality time is not the same as TV time. Make plans and engineer great evenings together whether at home or out.

- Earmark time just for the romantic connection between you. Dress up, look good, flirt, and take turns planning fun evenings for each other.

- We've learned it's never too late, as long as people are willing to move forward and work on their marriage.

SEXUAL INTIMACY: MOVING AWAY FROM SEXLESSNESS

MONA & DEREK

Dead Bedroom

"Typical. Derek's pissed again, because I refused to have sex tonight." *As she lay there pretending to sleep, Mona felt bad. It hadn't been that long ago that she was the only one who initiated sex. Derek was gorgeous, but he had let himself go. They never seemed to dress up anymore, or even go out to anything as basic as dinner. She would have settled for entertaining friends, gatherings at their house—any reason to be "on." Derek never seemed to care about setting up things with their friends, which annoyed her, but not as much as his lack of effort with her.*

When she had tried to be sexy, he seemed aloof, uninterested. Eventually, she didn't want to try anymore. She stopped noticing him and stopped caring. She focused on herself and the tasks at hand. They worked as good partners, but that was it.

Derek sighed loudly for emphasis. He knew something was up when Mona fell asleep so quickly. For so long Mona had criticized what she would call his deficit in romantic instinct. She said he never tried to have sex with her. She questioned aspects of his masculinity, just to come up with rationalizations to justify their lack of sex. Derek would readily admit that he wasn't the best lover. It wasn't that he didn't like sex, but he got into his head, still feeling like the fat kid he was in high school. He knew it had been months by tying events together, like a birthday, an anniversary, a vacation, or a night at a hotel. He didn't know what blocked him in between these times. He meant to plan more date nights and have their friends over, but exhaustion from work usually had him beat. It never felt intentional, but unfortunately Mona didn't see that.

Now that his new routine of exercise and clean living were paying off, he felt good, and even his sex drive had reappeared. Yet when he finally got his groove back, she was the one who was disinterested. While she never came out and said it, she evaded his attempts on a regular basis.

THE GREAT SEXUAL DECLINE

Married Roommates suffer in the bedroom. While your sexual intimacy usually starts out hot and heavy, with sex being more of a daily activity, time and habituation can have it fall back to several times a week. From there, bedroom activity can even shrink to multiple times a month. For many, it further dwindles to once a month, then it barely happens on birthdays and special occasions. If this sounds familiar, you are on the same track as most roommates.

A couple's broken connection usually inflicts its greatest damage on their sexual intimacy. Sex, passion, excitement, and even attraction greatly decrease when two people are not getting along.

When you don't see eye-to-eye and feel disconnected, you unfortunately do not want to be intimate. Conflict through fighting, escalation, and crossing the line can further solidify that feeling. The last thing you feel like doing when you are angry and disheartened is to be affectionate toward your mate. This easily creates a cascading effect, further downgrading your attraction, attention, and interest in one another.

SEX IS IMPORTANT

Sex plays an important role in connecting partners. Sexuality can unfold in many different ways, but for most people, the best sex feels organic and intuitive. There is a rhythm, a flirtation, a back-and-forth banter, and an intense hunger, all amounting to chemistry. When intensity is present in a relationship, you occupy one another's thoughts, you touch and stay close and largely aim to please by putting each other first.

Despite the many benefits of an intimate relationship, many couples allow for it to lose its luster. Even in the best relationships, sex can get boring over time. Being habitual creatures, you may use the same tricks again and again, losing some of the original appeal to your partner. Consequently, people passively allow passion disappear, letting familiarity and security inhibit desire.

When your sex life does taper off, it can affect you in devastating ways, bringing down your self-worth and self-esteem. It pains and hurts us to feel undesired and rejected. While interest and attraction may not be the reason for your partner's disinterest, when you are turned down, it is easy to personalize a rejection.

TIME FOR INTIMACY

Many couples who experience a decrease in intimacy report that they spend less time together. Other than our relationship, many other tasks demand our time. We become busy, even overwhelmed with the items on the to-do list. Struggles with proper time management and prioritizing can cause passion, romance, and even sex to get pushed lower and lower on the priority list.

Maintaining intimacy requires couples to make the time and effort to enjoy being with one another. All too often, couples fall into a pattern where the only time they spend with one another is silently side by side in front of the TV or in bed, before sleeping. This is the quickest way to become roommates, because as intimacy, connection, and sex decrease, sleeping or watching TV together is usually all we have left.

JIMMY & AURORA

What about Tonight?

Jimmy glanced over at Aurora sitting on the couch watching TV. While she didn't look very sexy with her Snoopy sweats and glasses, he felt that it had been a long time since he asked her for sex, so he figured he would try again.

"Wanna have sex?" he said playfully.

Aurora looked over at him as if considering it and said no yet again. She knew that it hurt him to hear that, but she had no physical desire toward him. Their relationship felt platonic. Her physical attraction toward him started waning as he lost his hair and gained more than twenty extra pounds around his gut. He knew what he had to do to get her interested again, she thought, as she put it out of her mind and refocused on the show they were watching.

Although Jimmy was crushed by her rejection, he didn't let on, but a few minutes later he got up and went to bed. He didn't sleep well that night, his thoughts circling around and around. He couldn't get past the deep rejection he felt—it affected his confidence and mood. It also made him extremely resentful that in order to sleep with his wife, he needed to hit the gym daily and get hair plugs. It was embarrassing to him and was such a turnoff that he vowed not to try with Aurora again. Fuck her.

WHERE DID THE ATTRACTION GO?

Attraction for one another is an important part of interest and sexuality. Through the course of a sometimes decades-long marriage, there will be times when physicality and attraction will be at an all-time high. There will also be downturns and times of low and lacking sexual fulfillment.

At the beginning of a relationship, you both usually devote some time and energy to your appearance. You style your hair, shave your legs, invest in new cologne, and dress up solely for each other. You do it for your mate to find you desirable and attractive. Over time, these practices can fade. While it is good to be able to just be yourself around your partner, the pendulum shouldn't swing solely in one direction. Physical desirability is an important part of maintaining attraction. When you cease putting in efforts to look your best—like wearing sweats with holes, and your favorite worn-out T-shirt from college—you are saying that you don't really care anymore. Again, there's nothing wrong with that if it is balanced out with some attempts to look your best. Unfortunately, Married Roommates have stopped balancing these out.

The aging process will see your and your partner's bodies go through normal changes, where parts will droop and sag, weight will be gained, and you may naturally let yourself go a bit. This should not stop you from caring about your appearance and trying for your mate, but it often does.

PETE & DIANA

You Changed and Not for the Better

Pete had always been fit. He wasn't necessarily an athlete, but he ate well and enjoyed keeping himself healthy. It wasn't for vanity, although he would be lying if he didn't admit that there was some truth to the accusations Diana would make. He liked nice things—especially stylish clothes, designer sunglasses, and even an expensive haircut. When he met Diana at a conference in Vegas, she had a rock-hard body and enjoyed the same upscale taste.

Because of these similarities, she had captivated him in ways that most women never did. Back then, she was so confident and sure of herself. But something shifted for her after motherhood. Physically things spun out of control, as working out and staying fit became less and less of a priority. Even worse, she lost her sense of self, seeming unsure of herself to the point where she let friends direct her opinions. She often put herself in a victim position in the relationship, saying things like, "I would gladly put on the weight all over again for my adorable babies." It drove him crazy. Her new neediness wasn't attractive. It made him lose interest, seeing her more as the mother of his children than an attractive and desirable partner.

Diana had always been described as a go-getter by the people who knew her. She had a fantastic resume, was well traveled, and well-informed. She never had problems in the guy department. She always dated the hottest guys in her hometown. During those years, her confidence was unshakable. She could go after anything she deemed worthy and would actually succeed in all her pursuits.

Diana was attractive, had a slender physique, and rarely gained weight. She ate well and liked dancing, hiking, and going for long walks with her dog. Marriage initially didn't change much in her daily life, but pregnancy did. Physically she felt horrible, and when her clothes stopped fitting, she spiraled into a low-grade depression (at least that was what her therapist told her). Her confidence seemed to fade with every pound gained, and instead of doing something about it, she consoled herself with food. She knew Pete was disgusted with her, as he wouldn't even touch her anymore.

NORMAL DOWNTURNS

There will be times in a couple's life when sex ebbs and flows; it wanes for instance during child-rearing, or when the wife experiences menopause. The husband, too, can experience low libido as he ages. These are normal downturns and are to be expected, but coming out of these ruts is not always automatic. Diana and Pete are an example of a couple who struggled to overcome these normal downturns and, as a result, experienced grave consequences to their intimacy and romantic relationship. Couples still have to actively engage and seek each other out for it to return to pre-rut levels, working against the disconnecting habits or routines that have formed during that time.

FACILITATING SEXLESSNESS

There will be times in your life when you face personal struggles outside of the relationship. These can definitely impact the sexual intimacy with your partner, despite lack of intention. Although it takes commitment, there are countless ways you can present the best version of yourself for your partner. Addressing dieting, unhealthy habits, depression, erectile dysfunction, or addiction can go a long way toward putting two people in the best position to reconnect.

Failing to address these individually can affect your marriage. While at first your partner could be understanding and empathic, failing to move the needle over time will not allow them to stay in a compassionate place.

As people grow older, get less sleep, and shoulder more personal and professional responsibility than ever before, exhaustion and personal self-care play a bigger and bigger role in the lack of intimacy. Couples resign themselves into this exhaustion once their duties have been fulfilled, preferring to get some downtime than to get sexual. This in turn facilitates their journey into Married Roommates, by allowing for a premature death to their sex life.

This phenomenon is aided by a lack of physical proximity, whether that is manifested by sitting on either side of the couch or the purchase of a king-sized bed, which serves to ensure that there is no accidental touching, cuddling, or playing footsies.

Married Roommates can simply cease to touch each other. While the longing for physical attention and affection may still be high, the distance stops you from asking for it and from pursuing it.

It is important to note that some partners believe sex can be optional. While they might not verbalize this directly to their partner, or even to themselves, their behavior clearly indicates that they deem it as unnecessary. These partners must understand that sex in marriage is not optional; it is an absolute must—unless *both* parties see lovemaking as a nonessential part of their union. This is non-negotiable in most marriages, but there are asexual partnerships where both parties agree that sex is not a necessity. However, if one party is indifferent and ambivalent while the other is needy, it spells trouble down the road.

Romantic relationships must be sexual; otherwise, they are by definition platonic. It is part of the job of being a husband and wife. Without it, in time, you find yourself in a marriage with little physical affection. Unfortunately, this state of sexlessness will not sustain indefinitely. Those partners who refuse to engage in it, steering clear through excuses and avoidance, are putting their marriage at risk.

DOUG & GINA

No to Sex, Yes to Porn

Doug couldn't help looking at the stairs, worried about Gina coming down and catching him in the act, masturbating. His mind rebelled against his fear. "It's her fault that I have to act like a sex-starved teenager and resort to sneaking around to watch porn." If she had sex with him like a normal wife, thoughts of having sex with other women wouldn't be consuming his waking hours.

Every time he reached for her or made a suggestive comment, she would shrug him off, always saying she was too tired or had a rough day at work. She had a million exhaustion-related excuses for why they couldn't be intimate. It embarrassed him, making him feel rejected and undesired. He knew Gina's views on porn—she considered it to be cheating. He didn't see it that way; he specifically watched porn because he did not want to cheat on his wife. He loved her despite their problems. But his sexual need was causing him to lose sight of that.

Although Doug brought it to her attention all the time, Gina wasn't concerned about sex. If she was honest with herself, she really didn't feel desire or arousal regularly, so it was easy to put it out of her mind. She knew it drove Doug crazy, but the fact that he was so horny all the time was his problem. She was sure he had a problem—maybe he was a sex addict. Which made it even more absurd when he asked her to talk to her doctor after seeing an ad for a shot that increased female libido. But why should she do that when he refused to help her? For years she had begged him to bring

her receipts from all the expenses on the small business they
ran together, and he wouldn't, leaving her the painful task of
trying to organize their company's finances without all the
supporting receipts.

MARITAL OBLIGATIONS: HIS AND HERS

Married Roommates can have duty sex. They fulfill their marital obligations to one another but in more of a transactional act, missing the sparks and intimacy. There is often no passion, no foreplay, and no cuddles. It happens, then it's over.

Once you've become roommates, intimacy sometimes feels like another forced obligation to be crossed off the list—nothing sexy, spontaneous, or passionate about it.

ILANA & SETH

Nothing New Here

As she dropped the kids off at her parents' house for their
weekly date night, Ilana wished that she could forgo the
whole event. She knew they needed to spend more quality
time together, but these evenings were so predictable and, if
she dared think it, boring. In attempts to work on their flailing
relationship, Seth suggested that they implement a weekly
date night, which was a good idea. Unfortunately, they always
went to the same restaurant, then the movies, then back
home to have sex. Seth didn't seem to have a lot of different
techniques in the bedroom. He never invested in foreplay to get
her into it. Instead, it was missionary position, wham bam, and

then let's get ready to go pick up the kids. There was usually no orgasm in it for her. Sometimes she felt so dissatisfied that she wanted to scream. She never shared these feelings with Seth, knowing that it would hurt him terribly.

At least he tried. Ilana just sat there turning her nose up and critiquing all his suggestions on how to improve their dead bedroom. He loved her, but she had a negative, sour attitude that made her unattractive. It was crazy, because even though they were now having sex regularly, he couldn't climax the last two times. Her stiff body and disengagement made him feel like he was fucking a corpse. She thought she could just lie there and let him get on with it, expecting him to go to town and not understanding how much of a turnoff her lack of participation created. He was ready to scrap this whole date night thing. He was sick of going through the motions.

Men and women are different. What we see most often in therapy is that women need intimacy from their partner to have a healthy sex life, and, conversely, men need a healthy sex life to feel intimacy and connection toward their mate. This is where the different gender approaches to intimacy and sex can often create an unfortunate cycle that literally pulls us further and further away from one another.

INFIDELITY AND OTHER DANGERS OF SEXLESS ROOMMATES

As pointed out earlier, the lack of sex leads to a breakdown in intimacy and emotional connection, leaving you susceptible to outside influences more than ever before. When you feel underappreciated and devalued by your significant other, it is easy for support to be found elsewhere, even if you aren't looking for it.

Where Did the Love Go?

Ana felt an iciness race down her spine as she reread Gerald's text: MISS YOU SUGAR. CAN'T WAIT TO SEE YOU TOMORROW. A dozen conflicting emotions pulled at her as she tried to digest the meaning of this text that was obviously not intended for her. He left that morning on yet another business trip, so it wasn't her that he would see tomorrow. More glaringly, it had been a long time since Gerald called her his sugar and said he missed her.

He was having an affair. She knew it deep down. She knew it before she tore through the house looking for clues, and before she spent hours on the computer seeking more information about his whereabouts. It almost made sense now, her mind thinking of a dozen unexplained absences, endless broken promises, and a web of lies holding their life together.

She knew they had problems. She knew he was unsatisfied sexually, as he told her often enough. But she hadn't realized that he would resort to this.

Infidelity is a very real and common consequence for Married Roommates. Some statistics suggest that in over a third of marriages, one or both couples admit to infidelity. That is a high number and indicates couples' vulnerability to cheating.

Unfortunately, we see couples struggling with the aftermath of infidelity too often. These days there are many shades of unfaithfulness, from just following inappropriate people on social media, or being engaged in naughty communication with others through the internet (stranger sexting), to having a full-blown affair.

From our perspective, many times infidelity is a by-product of relationship dissatisfaction. It's a slippery slope. Rather than an outright intent to step out of your marriage, you often flirt with danger by thinking that you can control the growing interest inside for another, rationalizing that they are just a friend, and that you could never be more than platonic.

It takes incredible willpower to pull this off with someone you actively spend time with and are attracted to, whether this happens at work, at a yoga class, or with another parent at your kids' school. All it takes is one intimate moment, proximity, or even alcohol to have you tumbling down that slope to an unintended destination.

Because women often have other women for emotional support and men generally do not, it leaves men more susceptible to finding emotional support in another woman. Men often find themselves talking to a coworker about general stuff, which, fueled by a tense home life, can easily cross the line into more inappropriate conversations about the struggles at home, like being unappreciated and the lack of sex. This is dangerous territory, as it sets the tone for an emotional affair, which many times is more damaging to a couple's relationship than a physical affair.

RYAN & LISA (& VICKI)

Coworker Connection

Ryan hung up the phone dejectedly. As usual the discussion with Lisa left him in despair. Her constant complaints about him were unwarranted and unfair. He stewed for a moment, took a couple of deep breaths, and headed to the office kitchen area for lunch.

Vicki was using the microwave when he walked in. Outside of work matters or polite conversations, Ryan rarely talked to people at the office. He felt it slowed his productivity, and he was always rushing to complete his tasks so he could rush home to what he sometimes referred to as his "second job."

When Vicki first started as the receptionist, he helped her to understand the complex phone system. It turned out her music taste mimicked his own, and through this shared interest they had developed an easy friendship.

Occasionally, Vicki would send him a link to a new song or band she liked, and he came to look forward to these emails. He found himself looking at his work email and refreshing it more often. He took lunches more frequently, going from never eating at the lunchroom, to once and then to daily sharing this time with Vicki.

He wasn't worried that it was inappropriate. They were both married. In time, their friendship became a place where they both vented about the challenges and lacking in their marriages, but that was it.

Over the weeks these vent sessions went deeper for both of them. They told each other every dark secret they ever had, including the traits that bothered them about their partners. The lunches became something they both looked forward to, and sometimes they would even meet at the restaurant across the street.

On the day Vicki discovered that her husband was having an affair, she and Ryan had already agreed to lunch at a Peruvian place down the street. She cried in the restaurant booth, Ryan at her side. She was visibly shaking, so he put his arms around her to console her. It seemed like only a second before they were kissing.

There is a high cost to resigning yourself to being roommates. Not only does a shell of your original relationship exist, roommate status may lead you to feel increasingly negative and burdened with your marriage. Untethered, you are susceptible to those in your environment.

While it may be a bit awkward to reengage sexually after a long hiatus, this weirdness doesn't last for long. Take into consideration that dealing with some uncomfortable moments is a small price to pay to get your relationship back on track. You can even greatly reduce the awkwardness by breaking the ice through humor, by being silly and playful with one another.

TIM & MANDY

Sexually Reengaging

Tim nervously put on the firefighter suit that he borrowed from his friend Jake, who was on vacation this week and wouldn't need it to run into any burning buildings. He felt weird and a little silly going commando underneath the heavy outfit, but he loved his wife and wanted to make it work.

He knew that Mandy was going to flip out when she saw this getup. She had a thing for firefighters, so he was sure she'd get a kick from his attempt at seducing her. They were going to therapy to work on their sex life and were committed to upping the sex, but nobody said it had to be boring sex, he chuckled to himself as he opened the bedroom door.

Mandy stared at him dumbfounded, then she cracked up. When she composed herself, she said, "Come here, you sexy nut." He jumped on the bed and she gave him the hottest kiss he had received in a long time. It was a good night; his efforts were definitely rewarded. He'd have to ask Jake where to buy one of those suits.

SOLUTIONS AND STRATEGIES

Removing the Bad

Removing the bad means acknowledging the state of sexuality in your marriage that unintentionally may have been put in place. Rejection, low sex drive (both sexes are guilty here), desire differentials, stress, exhaustion, boredom, habituation, body images, embarrassment, shyness—there could be *many* reasons behind a sexless marriage. But without your acknowledgment that any of these have become obstacles, nothing changes, and sexlessness does not improve.

Believe it or not, sex acts as a facilitator for even more sex, having a "use it or lose it" kind of quality. So make sex important. Take ownership and responsibility for your happiness together. Make your love life a priority.

Work against the obligatory/festive "occasion sex," which is mechanical and predictable, by training yourself to work on your relationship intimacy every day. Prioritize it—even if you have to schedule a time to be together. This could be a topic of discussion for talk time, where you brainstorm ways to intentionally create good sexual habits to combat some of the already entrenched bad ones.

Rebuilding the Good: Sexual Talk Time

Sexual issues could be compounded by a couple's lack of communication and openness when it comes to their own needs. Granted, sex is not an easy topic to broach, but feeling embarrassed or worried about hurting your partner's feelings should not be the reason to avoid these discussions. Talking about your sexual needs avoids repressing and minimizing sexuality, which only leaves you feeling frustrated and alone. Don't let hang-ups, insecurities, or negative thoughts push it back down. Turn sexual urges to each other instead of burying, ignoring, or releasing them alone.

Sex is important to discuss regularly. People come to the bedroom with different levels of sexual interest and drive, which change over time. Communicating your needs, interests, turn-ons, and turnoffs leaves your mate with something to go on to understand you sexually. Talking openly can *increase* desire and attraction, not to mention satisfaction, and ramp up your sexual repertoire beyond the basics. This does not have to be an uncomfortable conversation. You can be playful and make it fun.

Make increased desire and arousal a shared goal. Start by going to bed at the same time, encouraging physical closeness as your proximity to each other grows. Seek newness and novelty by discussing fantasies, asking questions, and suggesting new avenues for exploration of sexuality. Work on arousal not just to increase sexual tension, but to heighten openness and physical intimacy. Enhance your sexual repertoire by creating a sensual roadmap.

Avoid ingrained habits that keep you sexless. If she doesn't like it when you grab her body in an aggressive manner, accommodate and change. Don't just keep repeating what you have already been told is a turnoff. When he says that he wishes you would initiate sometimes, do it. Become the pursuer, not letting embarrassment or shame stand in your way.

WE SAY:

Arousal happens at different speeds for men and women. Men experience sexual desire in a more physically spontaneous way—the senses provide all the stimuli needed for instant desire. Arousal happens before any sexual activities even take place. Women, on the other hand, have their sexual desires awakened through those activities. Women's sex drive gets ignited by the dance before the final scene. It is the kissing, petting, and touching that creates the arousal in women. Getting your female partner truly engaged requires an investment in foreplay. It is worth noting that many women do not climax from intercourse, which makes foreplay even more important.

Strengthen Attraction

Work on your attraction to one another by investing a bit in your physical appearance. Start dressing up solely for one another. Do your best to look good for your mate by intentionally doing things that you know they like and appreciate. Actions such as flirting, complimenting, and simply courting your husband/wife go a long way toward strengthening attraction.

Initiate Intimacy

Make it a point to think good thoughts about the other person throughout your day. Knowing what they like and what makes them happy makes it easy to reach out with positive intent. Keep it going by leaving little notes in their car, sending an appreciative text, cooking dinner, or planning a special evening. Flirt with your partner, making eye contact, and intentionally touch them more often.

Engage Physically

Although our bodies are built for physical connection through sex, many times being in our head and intellectualizing it can rob us of the pleasure and sensations that come from being touched and seduced. Stop thinking. Focus on the sensations your senses are sending in and allow yourself to get lost in the moment.

Create physical closeness every day in these ways:

- Touching, holding hands, and hugging
- Choosing to sit near each other
- Kissing—not just the generic peck but the full, swapping-saliva kind
- Giving each other massages (shoulder, feet, full body)
- Calling each other with sexual thoughts or sexting

Learning to get comfortable around each other physically—undressing, sexual touching, using all your senses (sight, touch, sound, smell, taste) to engage your partner

> ## WE SAY:
>
> Pause and really look at your partner. Try to remember what it was like the first time you saw them naked or made love in a special location. Reflect on when you couldn't wait to unhook a bra or rub your hand gently across the front of his jeans.

QT or Date Night

Make date night sex night again. Although technically this might feel like scheduling sex, this was always the case when you were dating. Think about it. Wasn't date night also sex night?

Go out alone, without kids, friends, or family. Have something to look forward to. Take turns planning outings and then come home for the continuation of fun. Play around with being initiator. Set up surprise seduction scenes for each other.

Reintroduce passion through:

- Foreplay
- Nudity
- Make-out sessions
- Oral sex
- Mutual masturbation

When-at-Home Ideas

- Read erotica together.
- Play games with a sexual bend: anything from strip poker to strip bingo.

- Use newly acquired games: suggestive dice, erotic cards.

- Take a shower/bubble bath together.

- Watch X-rated movies together.

Out-and-About Ideas

- Make sure to flirt and touch one another.

- Visit a sex shop together and grab a few items to explore later.

- See a burlesque show.

- Meet each other out; invest in your appearance—go for a wow effect.

- Take the role-play a step further: pretend you don't know each other, create alter egos, and stay in character.

- Go to a drive-in and relive your youth by making out and necking in the car.

- Plan a weekend away and have loud hotel sex.

By this point you have most of the pieces needed to get a sense of where you can significantly improve your relationship and your sense of intimacy and connection. In the remaining chapters, we will look at bringing all this information together to implement change and be proactive in real life.

CHAPTER 7

KEY TAKEAWAYS

✔ Sexual intimacy and sex are integral, nonnegotiable parts of a romantic relationship.

✔ Without this "spark," roommates experience an unsatisfying routine-ness and emotional emptiness together.

✔ Married Roommates have a difficult time sexually. For most, sex has dwindled into infrequent and unsatisfying moments.

✔ While some are still having obligatory sex, it is often devoid of the intimacy, passion, and excitement that initially marked their sexual compatibility.

✔ Sex is crucial for maintaining an emotional connection, but we are often guilty of allowing it to grow stale and become a nonexistent part of our life together.

✔ Whether we like it or not, attraction is a big part of our physical desirability. When partners neglect their appearance and self-care, it affects attraction and sex life.

✔ There are natural ebbs and flows to a couple's sexuality—getting out of a downturn is not always seamless; it can be awkward and challenging to get back on track.

✔ Sexlessness and dead bedrooms have a cost; infidelity and divorce are very real and painful consequences on a couple and their family.

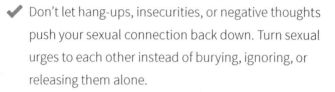 Make your love life and sexual connection a priority. While talking about sex is not always easy, it is necessary for you to get to know each other deeper.

Don't let hang-ups, insecurities, or negative thoughts push your sexual connection back down. Turn sexual urges to each other instead of burying, ignoring, or releasing them alone.

Engage physically by touching, kissing, and being close to one another.

Be creative in finding new techniques to enhance attraction and desirability.

PART III

OUT WITH THE OLD AND IN WITH THE NEW NORMAL

They slipped briskly into an intimacy

from which they never recovered.

—F. SCOTT FITZGERALD, FROM

THIS SIDE OF PARADISE

PUTTING IT ALL TOGETHER

AHEAD TOWARD 2.0

With some new tools and a reframe in how you see one another and your day-to-day interactions, you can create a new foundation for your marriage. Once completed, there will be two versions of your relationship. Version 1.0 will be the structure of the past, containing your old habits, poor choices, mistakes, ineffective tactics, and what you generally thought about relationships before you read this book.

Version 2.0 will include all your new efforts and behaviors that eventually form the habits that will reward you both. You are building a new foundation that is both structurally sound and long lasting. The movement to this new version is hardly ever a seamless transition. Along the way to sustainable change, you both may still be protective of your feelings and defensive of your behaviors. The leftover damage that trust violations perpetrated on your vulnerability will pop up periodically. This will happen more frequently in the beginning but decrease as you progress forward. Expect these periodic stumbles, and when they appear, do not allow them to trigger you and drag down all the progress you both made and will continue to make.

The truth is, in version 1.0, you both messed up. You lost control, called each other horrible and hurtful names, behaved inappropriately, and wounded each other deeply. This animosity will recede slowly as trust gets rebuilt. It will be there in the background, until one day, it just won't. When you have done enough work to heal one another, it will simply go away.

To fully realize the concept of a new version of the relationship, couples need a total paradigm shift that is more focused on the present and future, rather than on the transgressions of the past.

Since you can't change it or go back to that time, you must find a way to give each other a second chance to correct old mistakes. Learn to give your partner the benefit of the doubt, not letting old beliefs from the past always dictate your present and future. Forgiving and letting go of the hurt, which has served as a protective barrier, will allow you to truly be able to move on. To that end, you must be aware of and notice progress, to work against highlighting a leftover outlier. Doing so works against the entrenched and poor habits that you made as Married Roommates.

Catch yourself when you are set off by old triggers and look past minor infractions. Approach the traits that you would previously get angry or despondent about and ask yourself if it is really worth getting upset over.

If it is a small-scale annoyance, practice letting it go and moving on without making your partner aware of your feelings. Do so by talking yourself off the ledge by reminding yourself of the new efforts and the overall end game. Come up with some directive self-talk that corrects your reaction in real time. Tell yourself this:

- "This is not a big deal. In the long run, it won't even matter."

- "There's no need to get upset about this. He/she didn't mean to upset/hurt me. Just let it go."

- "If I want to have a happy marriage, I need to pick my battles. This was not intentional and it's not worth getting angry about."

If you must speak out on something that your partner said or did, or something that has happened, make sure that you think about the way you intend to present the issue or need. The goal here is to make it a positive and effective exchange, rather than just an avenue to deliver feelings. So use your cognitive abilities, rather than your emotional reactions, to help express your desire in a way that will be heard and understood.

Ask yourself this:

- "How can I say this in a constructive and kind way that won't hurt feelings and won't get my mate into a defensive mode?"

- "I want my partner to hear me. I will focus on presenting my needs and wants without blame on how he/she is not meeting those needs."

Being mindful and staying in the present creates a more optimistic future. Every time you have a good moment in the present, it goes toward healing the damage that the previous version created and helps put the past hurts and misunderstandings in the past, where they belong.

By threading the needle of positivity into each conversation and moment together, you take your relationship to the next level. Consistent use of these tools will change the faulty foundation and facilitate the paradigm shift to the newer 2.0 version, which lets you both win together, and definitely just feels better.

DO YOU WANT CHANGE?

It is not always easy to admit that you didn't have the right tools going into it, but marriage and any long-term relationships are their own unique animals. To be successful at it means that you may have to see and treat it differently than you historically have other relationships.

The motivation to change will only increase once you have some wins under your belt. Once some of the bad habits have been replaced by good ones, the dominos will begin to fall in the right direction.

It may be that one of you—probably the one reading this book— is more motivated toward change and may be spearheading the action toward version 2.0. That is great, as there is usually one person leading the charge forward. That person has either been assigned this job, or just took it on themselves. Although both genders can find themselves in this role, it seems like, statistically, it is a role often held by the woman in marriage. This doesn't mean that she does all the work, but in this case, she may be the unofficial or official leader and planner.

Your partner may be motivated right from the start, jumping in and implementing changes, shoulder to shoulder. It may also be that your partner is more resistant, claiming exhaustion, disinterest, or skepticism about the value of psychology and self-help books.

Even if this is true and you don't have a willing and motivated partner, don't despair and don't give up. That should not be a deterrent. It could be that as a starting point to get the other person's buy-in, you do the work on your own initially. Partners tend to buy in when they see the ways these changes impact them positively. By initially working to increase their hope and happiness, you get a more willing partner. If you start treating your mate well by changing your own approach, working toward respecting, complimenting, and giving them the benefit of the doubt, you will more likely convince them to come on board.

In the long run, in order for version 2.0 to be truly successful, it will require both parties' ongoing participation and investment. It will necessitate your partner to buy in at some point, but you may need to provide the carrot for him or her to do so.

Eventually though, you will both need the incentive to change what has just become habitual and easy. The proverbial carrot is your own positive behavior toward your mate, which will strengthen your partner's initiative, determination, and buy-in for change. Having positive reinforcements can ensure ongoing, active involvement and motivation to improve.

Division of Tasks Redo

Much resentment comes from the perception of responsibilities—who has more on their plate? Unfortunately, in some households it's not just perception—there's a very real imbalance in the load its partners carry. This is often one of the big grievances that can lead to divorce. It is time to look at your combined responsibilities and redo the list, redistributing your loads more evenly and fairly. Because life is fluid and is forever changing around us, you must revisit this discussion fairly often to keep up.

When both of the individuals get to the point where they see that the current system's flaws and unhappiness outweigh the difficulty of the transition to new habits, you will have created more unity for change, allowing new behaviors from each to create a new normal.

THE RELATIONSHIP BETWEEN INPUT AND OUTCOME

People generally have trouble connecting the dots between their choices and the direct consequences that occur as a result. Understanding the relationship between your input and outcome is crucial to success in any avenue.

Usually, instead of assessing the outcome, you give more thought to the intention. These two actions are not always directly correlated in a positive way. Your intent could be great, and it could still have a disastrous outcome. Positive intentions, used along with ineffective tactics, could set you up to continuously make the same mistakes.

It is a direct reflection of the old adage of doing the same thing over and over while expecting different results. This is a human trait in us all. It is normal, as our brain operates in an automatic fashion, sometimes without regard to the history of negative results attached to that choice. When you don't think in terms of outcome, you don't use foresight to curb or change present-day behaviors, even if you know unconsciously or through past experiences that these actions will play out poorly in the future. Failing to plan ahead and assess the real results of your actions is a minefield you can easily avoid.

Being aware of the consequences of your choices and behaviors is an important part of insight. This is a truism for everyone in all walks of life. Having insight as to the effectiveness of your efforts allows you to be less attached to your approach. If two parties in a marriage have different approaches to the same problem, why not choose the one that is most effective in outcome? It may require an adjustment, a change in approach for one of the partners, but if the outcome is better for both of you, doesn't it just make sense to do that instead of what isn't working?

We liken it to cooking. Imagine you are making a cake or soup, for example, and use certain ingredients to make your recipe, but the soup comes out tasting horribly bad. The next time you attempt to make this dish, you would probably change those ingredients or you'd end up disappointed with that same disgusting result. In the same way, if certain behaviors consistently lead to poor outcomes, it's time to recognize that fact, change those behaviors, and try something new.

BART & JACKIE

Mutual Satisfaction

Bart was excited for the game later today. Jackie was having some of her friends over, and he was going to have the afternoon free to indulge and watch the ball game undisturbed. He left for the office smiling. He received sweet texts from Jackie throughout the day, acknowledging his efforts for stopping at the new organic fruit stand (Jackie loved to make fresh juice) and cleaning the kitchen and both bathrooms ahead of tonight. He knew she wouldn't have the time to get the house organized, so he took the stress off her plate by doing it himself. It was no big deal. In fact, since he began to do these small gestures toward Jackie, he had a much happier and more appreciative wife. It paid off. He made a note to call the pizza joint down the street to preorder a pie for Jackie and the girls on his way home.

Jackie was looking forward to tonight. It had been a long time since she had her friends over for a girls' night. She had a great deal to do to get the house ready for company. When she got home and saw the clean kitchen and the fruit and veggies Bart had purchased earlier sitting on the counter, she was delighted. The change in his behavior for the past few months was incredible. It made her think about him as she used to when they were first dating. Jackie even missed him when he was at work, and that had not happened in a long time. She kept thinking about how awesome it was that he stopped at the fruit stand, and she hadn't even asked.

When she saw the clean bathrooms and realized that she could just relax for the rest of the afternoon, she was so appreciative that she sent him a series of excited texts to let him know. She couldn't believe how amazing he was being. Thoughts about how she could make it up to him were swirling in her mind for the rest of the afternoon.

Applying This to Your Marriage

The truth is that you know your mate—what they like and don't like. You know what makes them happy and what makes them furious. Using this information proactively gets you better outcomes, and you both win. Knowing one another should help this process along, as you can easily create scenarios where you provide carrots for each other just by going out of your way for one another.

When making decisions based on effectiveness, you end up taking action and responding less from a place of emotional reactivity and more from an intellectual capacity to forecast the outcome. This inevitably will result in a win-win for both parties. When your spouse goes out of their way to do nice and thoughtful acts, naturally you want to give back, to acknowledge these efforts and reciprocate. This technique can be used in any context for physical and emotional needs. For most, there isn't anything to lose but an entrenched and unproductive reality, filled with routines that don't please either of you. The wins, however, could hold the secret passage to gaining all the benefits you've ever wanted and needed from your mate.

JANEY & MARLA

Committed to Change

Janey and Marla both had stressful and demanding jobs. Even after work, they found themselves tightly wound. Irritation poured out of them like a fountain the minute they walked in the door.

It seemed that their evenings together were just a continuation of their workday, as they would both vent and complain as they ate dinner, then just go back to work on their laptops. Sometimes they would do so in the same room side by side, but more often, they found themselves in different rooms after a fight over a forgotten detail around the house left them angry. Marla was usually on the balcony, working on her laptop, while Janey did the same in the bedroom.

It just became their normal routine, until they decided to make a change. Marla was the one who initially brought up her unhappiness with their home life, which led to some positive discussions about poor habits that they both could agree on. Janey and Marla came to understand that they both made work a priority over each other, which was never their intent, and vowed to make some tweaks in their routine. Both shared their feelings and made suggestions about what they wanted to see more of. Through calm discussion they realized that they made their time together at home overly negative, through venting and discussing work stressors.

At therapy, they made a deal that work would not be discussed for at least an hour after they got home, no matter what. They also decided that they needed to turn the tide on the negativity that they felt toward one another, by saying one complimentary thing about each other every day, no matter what. It was actually easier than they thought.

The new rules were helpful. When they got home from work, they would take time to sit together, checking their work stress or frustrations at the door. Instead they made a point to spend a few minutes sharing something positive that happened or that they were feeling about their lives.

The phone reminders that they both initially set up were instrumental in helping them to stay positive. Being mindful helped shift their engrained habits in the right direction. After a while, they found that they didn't even need the reminders; just the good energy around the house was enough to reinforce this change.

YOU WANT IT, NOW CHANGE IT

Change happens in real life. Take time to discuss and implement new strategies, and change will happen. Ideally this will become routine, and through reinforcement it will become second nature.

Acknowledge that you have developed bad habits, realizing that the routines, distractions, survival loops, and justifications that push you toward being logistical roommates must simply stop. The goal is that conversations and accountability established in your talk time will create a new roadmap—one that will pave the road to version 2.0.

Researcher Phillippa Lally supposes that it takes, on average, sixty-six times doing something to create a new habit or behavior. We're talking about two months for changing a bad habit into a good one.

Commitment Roadmap

Getting there will require that you work at change every day. This doesn't have to be a time-consuming endeavor. Initially making change would entail the same time you devoted to each other before, just with a new, positive twist. The time that was formerly given to bad habits—arguing, disagreeing, stewing, and being upset—now gets converted into positive, building moments.

To get there you must commit to these practices:

- **Practice bouncing back more quickly.** If you have a disagreement, cut down the time that you previously spent recovering and licking your wounds. This might require you to not let ego or hurt feelings keep you from initiating a shorter time line to the apology and subsequent forgiveness. The upshot to this intentional resolution is that it sets the groundwork for forgiveness becoming a more intimate affair. Kissing and making up can motivate you to end unnecessary squabbles.

- **Learn to dip, duck, and pivot together.** You'll *always* have problems and issues hurled at you. But if you work together, you can nip these in the bud, problem solve, and make needed decisions more successfully.

- **Make the time for continued change.** It is crucial to set aside space in your schedule for both talk time and quality time weekly. Talk time is used to get on the same page and remove old entrenched patterns. The time in between these meetings is your practice of it—the dress rehearsal, if you will. It is your time to brainstorm and build new habits and tasks, set optimistic goals, and commit them into your day-to-day routines through the use of a calendar and ongoing reminders.

- **Start at the place that you both need to.** Whatever is most pressing to you can be worked on first. You can go as slow or as fast as you both agree to.

- **Break these big ideas down into small tasks.** No need to become overwhelmed by all the work you need to do. Start slowly. Pick one or two tasks to focus on. Once you have reached an acceptable level of success, add another, and when you are ready for it, go for another.

Use of Calendars and Reminders

Make a point to write down your new commitments to behavior or habits. You will need reminders to keep you on track to avoid falling back into the old routines. The repetition will soon make it so that the reminders will not be necessary, but at the onset of your journey out of the roommate reality, they are crucial.

Once you agree upon what you are focusing on, decide what your reminders will be. This is an extremely important step of accountability, which should not be skipped. Remember, the brain doesn't like change and that you behave in largely automatic ways. If you don't have a system for placing this new behavior into routines to basically force your brain to utilize these new habits, it simply won't, and you will slink right back to the status quo that was not working. Don't just trust your brain to be your secretary. It won't work.

To help maintain your progress, do this:

- Hang a new chart up on the fridge or other accessible areas.
- Get a whiteboard.
- Use a shared calendar.
- Program reminders into your phone.

WE SAY:

Repetition and consistency make a behavior habitual and automatic. Until it becomes second nature, which eventually makes thinking or remembering unnecessary, you need a way to remind yourself.

Increase Efforts

Send texts, verbalize or even put thankful sticky notes in each other's car, makeup bag, computer, medicine cabinet—the list is endless. Here you are actually reinforcing the change by thanking or acknowledging your partner for their efforts—not to mention giving your partner much-needed positive attention and affection. It may feel awkward and disingenuous to both of you at first, but since you do truly feel for your partner, the only reason it does feel a little off is because it is a new, unexpected behavior.

Don't let negative emotions infect these gestures. Remind yourself what is at stake and what you are fighting for. Reframe your own negative thoughts by telling yourself that all these actions are necessary to get the relationship you want.

Eliminate Distractions/Crutches

Technology—texting, emails, and posting on social media—has given us artificial crutches to get through the day. These habits have become so common and useful to life that they have begun to replace real moments. Losing precious time and real life moments in screens, whether television, laptops, or phones, is something you have to consciously recognize and want to change.

Throughout your development, there were other authority figures present to enforce limits and create boundaries. You had parents, teachers, and coaches to create the structure of life, helping you navigate the rights and wrongs, the good and bad, the beneficial and hurtful. You may even still have this structure dictate your professional life, as management and bosses create your work boundaries, schedule, and routines. But nowadays who parents your personal life? Who forces you to manage and maintain good friendships? Who monitors your habits and helps you see when you've crossed the line into unhealthy and possibly damaging ones?

The responsibility lies within you.

You must decide on those boundaries, understanding which actions are valuable and which end up sabotaging you and stealing your precious time. Assess and really decide if screen time is dominating areas of your life negatively. Be honest with yourself if technology is taking away from being present in your relationship.

As rewarding as technology can be, you have to be the boundary enforcer, the one who limits the candy and forces the broccoli. In the same way that failing to take care of your body will eventually work against you, failing to take care of your relationships will also have the same undesired outcome.

Check in First

When couples reconnect after time apart, whether that is after a day at work or more substantial time, they need to get into the habit of checking in. Don't just walk in the door with a day's worth of anxiety and angst, easily projecting and unleashing it onto each other. The shitty day, road rage, or anger finds an easy target in each other, where it does not really belong.

Find a way to individually deescalate from your day, taking time on your commute to let go of any stressors and not bring them home. Healthy transition methods include these:

- Play your favorite music.
- Listen to an uplifting podcast.
- Do some mindfulness exercises.
- Meditate.
- Sit in your driveway for ten minutes and just decompress from your day.

When you walk in the door, make it a point to not just be business as usual. Make greeting each other a treasured moment of connection. Stop whatever activity you are doing and make yourself physically present by using direct eye contact and genuinely inquiring into your partner's well-being and mental head space.

Do so verbally by pausing to really ask, "How are you?" and then listening.

The person being asked probably doesn't know how they really are at that moment, and the person asking obviously doesn't either.

Avoid the facade answers of "fine" or "good" and go for deeper, more descriptive one-word adjectives such as "I am happy/excited/stressed/worried/overwhelmed/sad/frightened." Your mate can't know if you are walking in as a ticking time bomb, in need of gentleness and comfort, or space to deescalate and get a few moments of solitude, if you don't tell them. Make sure that there is nothing from the external world that may unfairly color your present interaction. Resist bringing the baggage of the day home with you, but when it's been one of those days and you can't help it, ask for a venting moment (revisit chapter 4).

Protect the Relationship

Be vigilant and hyperprotective of this effort for positive change, including your time together. Don't let anything get in the way of this change, which could be unknowingly sabotaged by others. Remember that the people in your life are inherently biased because they love you. If you share your pain about your partner's behavior, you cast a shadow on their image. You will go on to forgive and forget, but your loved ones will not. Protect your spouse from these natural human tendencies.

Keep It Private

Changes occurring in your relationship don't need outside pressures or opinions to muddy the water. Keep the changes and updates to yourself, discussing issues only with your partner (or an outside professional, of course). Protect the relationship and one another by reducing those in the know. Some issues are meant to be private. Keep it that way.

Be a Friend

Elevate the importance of this relationship. Speak about your marriage in glowing terms, only highlighting the good and valuable. Have one another's back, even with your own families, your kids, or just life's demands. Ask one another what is needed for them to feel protected, and then use what you learn to build this trust between you.

You are a team—just you two—so act like it.

CHAPTER 8

KEY TAKEAWAYS

- ✔ You now have the tools to build a new foundation and fortify your connection successfully.

- ✔ Doing so creates a 2.0 version of your relationship that does not have the same poor habits dragging it down.

- ✔ Note that there will be slipups until old behaviors are extinguished and eliminated completely—those outliers must be seen for what they are, a mistake and not necessarily a backslide to old times.

- ✔ Accept that in version 1.0 you both messed up. You hurt each other and made mistakes, and most were not done intentionally. Couples must learn to focus on their present and future, letting go of the past and the emotional entanglements caught up in it.

- ✔ Work to give your partner the benefit of the doubt and catch yourself before you get reactive and are off and running with your own assumptions. Talk yourself off the ledge when dealing with minor infractions, and remind yourself that marriage means compromise.

- ✔ Spend some time thinking about your delivery. Is that how you would like your partner to address you? Try to do better, being nicer and more considerate when delivering your messages.

✔ Don't despair if you have an unmotivated partner; do the work first and see if they jump onboard once your behavior changes toward them first.

✔ Change happens in real life. Work together to understand the connection between your behaviors and the outcomes. If you seek different outcomes, it is time to look at the behaviors that got you there.

✔ Be committed to change. Start by implementing changes and being consistent about it through built-in reminders and scheduled moments.

✔ Many protective elements can strengthen a relationship: checking in, eliminating distractions, being friends, and limiting your shares about personal issues. Make these baseline routines in your life, and you will protect the relationship for years to come.

THE PLAN FORWARD TOWARD 2.0

REAL-LIFE IMPLEMENTATION

While you may have accepted the reality of married life, truly accepting adulthood goes a step further. Many may think that this is a given when you become an adult, part of the territory, but that unfortunately is not always the case.

The insight necessary for true success in adulthood means recognizing that you, and only you, have the power to make even the hardest or most challenging reality into one that is peppered with contentment, excitement, and happiness.

Although there are more responsibilities and challenges in life, married life is accompanied by having far more control over the outcome. You have more power today than you ever had. You have the ability to navigate the impact of reality by changing your mindset, and at the same time driving your goals forward. When you take control of your perspective, nothing anyone else does can impact your choices for long. You always find a way forward by not letting problems weigh you down or keep the solutions elusive.

Shift to an active versus a passive approach to life, embodying the proverbial adage of "when life gives you lemons, make lemonade." Whether it comes to your marriage, family, work, or progression in life, having a positive can-do attitude toward it just works to strengthen you and inevitably improves the outcome.

PLANNING FORWARD

As we previously discussed, human beings are creatures of habit, set in their ways, programmed to routinely do the things they do. Without even thinking about it, you automatically follow an internal pattern of the same built-in drills day after day. The bad habits you have created individually and together play out that way, automatically. They become who you are, even without intent, transforming into familiar second nature just through repetition.

Eradicating these patterns requires that better habits come in their place, but it must be done manually. You will need to create these and use the same mechanism of repetition to make them built-in, automatic habits. Using the reframes and tools provided earlier will help you to form the foundation for healthy habits needed to forge this new path. Repeated use of these new behaviors will work to replace the old, ineffective ones.

That is just the beginning. Using this ability to collaborate does not just limit you to replacing bad habits. It can help you go even further, toward anything you might dream of achieving.

Just by getting into the habit of planning together, you open previously shut doors. With intent, motivation, and organization, couples can soon begin to realize their joint and compounded strength can make anything a reality. Whether that entails a move across the country, a trip around the world, building a pool, opening a business, or renovating your bedroom, these upgrades and quality-of-life elevators can be back in play.

Having plans and direction will always propel you toward achieving the goals you aspire to reach. You may not have had wins with one another in such a long time that you stopped believing these were even possible. Once couples build a good baseline of communication, and feel unified as true teammates, then the planning and strategizing together gets easier and, believe it or not, more fun. The collaborating couple can look into a future that hasn't happened and unify to create the roadmap there together, moving steadily past each obstacle in their way as teammates, to make it happen.

SHARED GOALS

Shared goals can offset some of the drudgery from the shared life. While it is fun to engage in fantasy-based dreams of a future together, these ideas don't just have to stay in the realm of unfulfilled fantasies. They could be made into real life, materialized through action and roadmaps to get you there.

These types of goals are extremely important for onward movement, but also for our shared hopes and dreams. It can help us move from static and predictable places that have sapped our fun and joy to incredible new heights together, leading to more enjoyable time and an ability to reward ourselves for all the hard work.

To create real-life change together, planning forward is a must. What you do not plan generally does not happen. You are just too busy and scheduled for events to just occur spontaneously without specific input and determination. By creating short- and long-term goals in every arena of life, couples can open up new possibilities for a future that they never thought or imagined possible. Making plans for the immediate and far-off future allows for targeted strategizing and uses your compounded ambition and motivation to push forward together.

No plan can be too big or too small if you work together to create goals and identify the steps to get you there. Breaking the long-term goals into smaller, more digestible tasks that can be completed weekly or monthly can help propel you toward not only cementing great new habits together, but making your dreams happen as a result of them. Addressing longer-term goals in smaller forms gives you immediate gains and reinforces progress forward. The small steps each person completes week by week can become massive strides after a few months.

This type of collaboration lets you plan and build success, happiness, adventure, and excitement into your life where it was missing before. By not just winging it together, you create a system that allows you to win, not just drudge through life in a parallel fashion. Doing so gives couples something positive to look forward to.

DAPHNE & ELI

Projecting Life Forward

Since their communication improved through use of the code word and talk time strategies, Daphne and Eli had more time together. Previously they had spent so much time being upset and angry, which took away precious time to do anything else. With that behind them, they made a point to spend more time together doing a hobby both could enjoy. They took up sailing, which grew into a passion for both of them. Daphne came up with the idea of purchasing a small sailboat and storing it in the closest marina. It was a fantasy, but one that they both dreamed about so frequently that five years later, it became a reality. They had saved every last dime, took on extra jobs, and did an incredible amount of research, but they made their dream come true.

THE PRESENT CARVES OUT THE FUTURE

What you do today helps pave the reality of tomorrow. Once you decide on shared goals going forward, use your weekly talk time to clarify what change needs to be made today and every subsequent day until you achieve your goal.

Planning together should be seen as an organizational tool to not only keep your head above water today, but as the method to set the course toward improvement you will want to achieve tomorrow.

Staying committed to a weekly time to talk can keep couples focused and organized on building their relationship, their family, their home, their career, and their own self-growth. The proactive approach can literally make anything happen. It can be used with regard to planning nights out, vacations, home improvements, quality family time, time with friends, or career/life changes. If you approach this discussion with an open mind, focused on moving forward, not just looking backward, *anything* is possible.

Working as a team is what gets you the life you want. Jointly brainstorm and break down the habits and tasks you will need to take to actually get there.

If you decide that having a neater and more organized home is a goal, what would be the actual steps needed to achieve it? Outlining the habits that you need to support a new goal is critical to its success. In this example, committing to a new routine where you both devote fifteen minutes every evening to putting clothes and clutter away would help to achieve the goal of having a neat house.

It takes intention to make action occur. Just coming up with a goal without acting on it is futile. It won't work because you will automatically reset to your factory hardwiring if you do not make an actionable habitual plan. Come up with your goals and the habits that must be attached to them for success. Here are some common goals in action:

- **The goal is to promote more conversation and connection.** The habit supporting this goal could be limiting use of devices during dinner. It could also be implementing a weekly game night or a rule of no TV on certain nights.

- **The goal is to create a healthier lifestyle.** The behaviors to be targeted could be cooking dinner together, joining a gym, walking around the neighborhood at night, or going for hikes multiple times a week.

- **The goal is to be more social.** The habits to get you there could be organizing a monthly get-together with friends, hosting gatherings in your home, being more social at birthday parties, or taking a class together.

- **The goal is to improve your intimacy and improve your love life.** The habits that will get you there may be to go to sleep at the same time, bring in a weekly babysitter, and sit next to each other on the sofa, touching and holding hands.

FRIENDSHIPS: SUPPORT SYSTEMS

Although many couples may retain individual friendships from a prior time, it is crucial that they also seek out friends who can serve as family friends. There is no substitute for a strong support system, and having like-minded friends who are in the same boat or act of life is such a critical part of your infrastructure. Without it you are going at it alone. Doing so leaves you vulnerable, without anyone to normalize life with or vent to, which can be undeniably challenging.

While social media has given us a false representation of what the world is doing, developing real support systems, with real-life friends, can create normalization and a safe outlet to vent and share war stories about some of the more challenging and draining stages that you both go through.

In addition to pursuing friendships in real time, we encourage clients to be more open and honest within their friendships, by openly discussing employment stress and marriage or parenting issues with those friends they trust. If your friends can be vulnerable enough to open up and get past the facade, they will be able to tell you about something obnoxious their kid did, or that they are roommates too, without having to excuse or rationalize it. Those are the people with whom you can share a demeaning or embarrassing experience at work without worrying about receiving a pearl-clutching expression. Remember, most of the people you know are going through the same experiences behind closed doors, so it is highly likely that they too are actually roommates pretending. Hearing your frustrations will most likely be a freeing experience for them as well.

VACATIONS: OFF-TIME

Married Roommates sometimes underestimate the value of vacations as a healing and bonding time for spouses and families. Many times, couples do not take vacations due to money concerns, but this could be a surmountable obstacle if you worked together creatively to find low-cost options and save your money monthly to that end. Effective planning allows you to turn this situation around.

Organization will assist you in carving out better systems and will lead to better time management and improved results. That will inevitably lead to a reduction in anxiety, more frustration tolerance, and a better overall mood.

THE VALUE OF FUTURE PROJECTIONS

There will come a time when you have life back to yourself. That time comes along when the demands of life slow down, when your kids have been successfully launched into the world, and when the building of a career is now behind you. Expenses and duties will decrease naturally, and your time, both alone and together, increases dramatically. We are talking about Act III, and although those days may seem far off, you will get there. If you use your ability to dream about this time, you will also be able to manifest and control this future together.

Couples need an avenue for hope—a place that allows them to get back to dreaming together of the future they want. Using your imagination and living in the world of pretend, if only for a moment, is a powerful connector for two people.

Much of the early years of your time together was spent talking about and building these projections together. Talking about the names of your future kids, the back-and-forth discussions on building a house on the shoreline, and what to do with your imagined lottery winnings are all examples of this powerful tool's ability to sow the seeds of hope and dreams.

The ability to envision a happier time is an important coping mechanism. You easily called upon this skill as a child when it helped you to see the magic in the world. Too often, adulthood robs you of that joy of fantasy. Having this ability to imagine and fantasize is an important survival mechanism. It helps in planning and strategizing forward, providing the motivation to push through the mundaneness of adult reality.

While that ability is still there, briefly appearing in daydreams and sexual reveries, your own individual musings are often not merged with those of your partner. When those daydreams come together, you can imagine your journey forward unencumbered, wandering past the limitations of reality in thoughts of what you will do with the money once you win the lottery, and what you will do if your business takes off, and where you will go once the kids have their own families and you retire.

The idea behind future projections is not just unification and bonding. It so happens that fantasizing together helps you manifest what you now see as unreachable and make those dreams actually attainable. Seeing a goal in your mind's eye creates direction and builds opportunities and possibilities that may not currently exist. Doing so gives couples a purpose, helping you both grow in the right direction. Don't just use your imagination to get through the tough, lean times, or for problem solving. Use imagination to create the pathway toward a more spectacular and limitless destination.

SONNY & JAN

Together Forever

Even though they had been together for thirteen years, their basic court ceremony had always been a sour spot. They used to be so angry and argumentative with one another that he just couldn't see the future playing out well. But since they went to therapy, it was like a new relationship. They understood each other more and fought less. He was so in love with Jan that he wanted to give her the wedding of her dreams. She deserved it for sticking around and not giving up on them.

He told Jan that his brother was ready to propose to his longtime girlfriend and needed her help with the plans for the wedding. What she didn't know was that she was planning her own wedding redo. The day she found out went down in history as the best day in both their lives.

These future-focused discussions could help you get to know each other again and see the softer side of one another. It also detours you away from the boring, repetitive roommate discussions about the house, work, friends, and kids.

Having lighthearted conversations and a what-if back-and-forth banter allows you to be silly, playful, and engaging with one another. It takes the heaviness and stiffness away, creating a space for fun, and inspiring you to believe in one another again.

Such dreams can start with the achievable and move toward the harder to achieve. Having some successes under your belt will make you more apt to continue to stay motivated. Here are some suggestions:

- Create a shared bucket list.

- Look at a world map and determine places you'd like to one day visit.

- Brainstorm all the skills you would love to do/ learn (such as skydiving, learning French, taking a cooking class).

- Make a wish list of projects you would like to do in your home (for example, adding wallpaper to the den or upgrading a bathroom).

- Plan the perfect retirement.

You can use what you learn about each other's dreams to make your partner happy, to give one another the best gifts, and to literally make what they imagine into a reality, as Sonny did for Jan in the example you just read.

We love it when we hear couples talk about the future. It means that future projections have started and that they are back on track to collaborating together. These are things they are going to have to see, prior to manifesting them in real life.

Once again, patience and a positive outlook will be required, but consistent collaboration, without pressure to conform, will bring about positivity and a can-do attitude.

FINE-TUNE YOURSELF TOO

While couples can take many steps to improve their relationship and develop healthier habits, there are also individual behaviors and attitudes that, if improved, will compound positive change faster than you think.

Your individual coping skills could be healthy or not, and assist you in keeping your head above water or helping you to go under— from faulty and rigid beliefs that only end up sabotaging yourself, to insecurities and fears, crippling doubts, and anxieties. You could have a short fuse, be easy to anger and quick to explode, or have little patience for the mistakes of others in your life. You could be overly emotional, needy, and demanding or self-absorbed and disinterested in the wants and needs of others. In an insightful adult life, these issues must be acknowledged and addressed, or they just end up sabotaging and torpedoing your progress forward.

Taking care of yourself avoids the trap of projecting your unhappiness on your mate. As much as having a partner to go through life together with is a benefit, it can also create a situation where your expectations from one another are extreme and set everyone up for failure. Your partner cannot wear all the hats that you project onto them, as it is hard to be someone else's everything—best friend, lover, confidante, soul mate, troubleshooter, and parent.

Self-care is an extremely important concept in Act II, as many times all your resources go to your job, your children, and the demands of life. It is all too common for couples to just stop the activities that keep them healthy, happy, and motivated because they believe that all their free time must go to the family or to their job. Hobbies, friendships, and support systems can thus dwindle into nonexistence during the toughest chapter of life, when you need them most.

When your own self-care or mental health is compromised, you cannot bring your best self to your marriage or family. While your internal voice may rationalize and convince you otherwise, it is important to validity test your own thoughts against reality. If you keep telling yourself that you are not depressed, but the evidence of a downgraded existence is evident in you sleeping more, eating less, and not wanting to do anything with your kids or mate, it is important that you take note and seek solutions.

No one is perfect. Each partner may come to the table already with preexisting or developing issues. When they refuse to acknowledge or fix these issues, it will just work to derail you both. These issues can include:

- Depression
- Anger/reactiveness
- Negative body image
- Insecurity
- Anxiety
- Laziness

Your own past could have left you scarred and traumatized. Sometimes it is due to events that have occurred within the relationship, and sometimes it is about the events that predate our relationships. It may be hard to hear or accept that these more individual issues will impact your marriage and that, inevitably, your failure to deal with them may make life much more challenging for you individually and as a couple.

While initially your mate could be supportive, loving, and understanding regarding the presence of these issues, if left unfixed, at some point they will cease being so. You will have to be the one to take action and facilitate initiative. Doing so is good for your mental and physical health—and ultimately good for your relationship and family. By looking at your own individual habits and coping skills, you can implement a better lifestyle, utilizing exercise, healthy eating, and stronger support systems.

TO SUM IT ALL UP

Marriages don't just affect the couple. Marriage has a profound effect on children and families, and on communities and societies as a whole. We hope this book will help couples who find themselves as Married Roommates discover strategies for change. Our message here can also be used proactively for couples who want to take heed of these issues and, by becoming aware of the pitfalls, bypass them altogether. As with most important and valuable messages, preventive measures are more effective than reactive ones. Trying to get yourself or the relationship back on track once it falls off the grid is much harder than to do the maintenance work necessary to keep it from getting there.

Dealing with increasing unhappiness and negativity while kicking the can down the road will ensure that your ability to be preventive disappears and all you will have left is reactiveness. It saddens us to get calls from potential clients who are five years too late. When we hear that relationships are hanging by a thread and that we are their last hope, to us it is an indicator that the preventive work was not done—that couples haven't taken care of the relationship and maintained it in a way that created options until it fell into crisis.

This book can offer a lot of normalizations, as well as tools and insight, to change the things we would like to change, but sometimes you may need additional support in the form of therapy. A skilled therapist can help you understand and clear the obstacles that still stand in your way.

Although this book has taken a look at the most pressing issues facing Married Roommates and provided the fundamental tools needed for success, the rest of the journey toward change depends on what you do with the new knowledge. If you start taking baby steps, then this change becomes a reality. Although you may be scared, uncertain, and unsure, you can link hands and go through it together, step by step, until you reach success.

We are rooting for you.

CHAPTER 9

KEY TAKEAWAYS

✔ You have incredible power to change your life if you tap into its source.

✔ Moving from a passive perspective to an active one means you take control of what you feel and what you do, intentionally directing yourself where you want to go a step at a time.

✔ You have the ability to navigate the impact of reality by changing your mindset, and at the same time driving your goals forward. When you take control of your perspective, nothing anyone else does can impact your choices for long. You always find a way forward by not letting problems weigh you down or keep the solutions elusive.

✔ Getting into the habit of projecting your life forward with your goals can lead to incredible gains both individually and together. But you must work together as a well-oiled machine.

✔ With intent, motivation, and organization, couples can soon begin to realize their joint and compounded strength can make anything a reality.

✔ Create short- and long-term goals together to propel yourselves forward and keep you accountable. Making plans for the immediate and far-off future allows for targeted strategizing and uses your compounded ambition and motivation to push forward together.

✔ This type of collaboration lets you plan and build success, happiness, adventure, and excitement into your life where it was missing before.

✔ Planning together should be seen as an organizational tool to not only keep your head above water today, but as the method to set course toward the improvement you will want tomorrow.

✔ Promote support systems in friendships and social connections.

✔ Get away from it all and just connect. See vacations as a necessity (even the smallest staycations), using this as a time for bonding and having fun.

✔ Take care of yourself individually, so you can be there to care for each other.

Thank you for taking the time to read *Married Roommates.* *If you found the book to be helpful, please take a minute to review it on Amazon and help us get the word out.*

AFTERWORD

The story does not end with *Married Roommates*—it's only the beginning. Once that core foundation between its participants is strong and steady, most couples will be ready to build on top of that footing.

While marriage does not come with its own instruction manual, neither does the next big challenge of life—becoming parents. It is probably the hardest, most demanding, and most important job in the world, yet most of us don't really know what we are doing. We are all winging it—sometimes successfully, sometimes not.

Parenting is a job that never ends; it tests every ability and skill you have and demands that you take on different roles at different times. It is a massive undertaking. In addition to your kids' basic needs, you are responsible for their education, physical health, and emotional and social development. All of this is hard enough, but when two parents pull in different directions when it comes to raising children, parenting becomes almost impossible.

As most soon realize, being consistently on the same page is extremely challenging. Although you may understand the importance, you may not know how to be a united front when it comes to your kids. It is too hard, and you are too exhausted and overwhelmed. While you try your best, you can come up short. It is easier to just give up when you get stuck.

Our follow-up book—*Married Roommates with Children*—will help couples get and stay on that same page, offering them the tools to create and maintain the discipline and structure needed to raise happy, confident, and successful kids in a loving and safe home.

Join our mailing list at marriedroommates.com to learn more.

ACKNOWLEDGMENTS

The most important and heartfelt acknowledgment we can give is to one another. Only we can know the bends and turns on the road we walked together. There were great days and shitty days. Ones where patience was low and disinterest was high. Despite it all, we kept walking and pushing forward the best way we knew how.

Our kids deserve a special shout-out for tolerating busy parents who don't always have the time and energy that they'd like. We hope that we are showing our kids the truth—that life is hard, but if we work hard, and work together as a team, we all win. We hope this book has inspired you to take that same approach.

Thank you to all the people who helped make this book a reality, from the family members to the professionals who accompanied us on this journey. You illuminated the right path at many confusing junctions. We appreciate it and hope to call on your strengths and skills again sometime soon.

To the clients who walk through our door, sometimes at a low point in life, worried and scared, thank you for entrusting us with your stories and your pain. You have helped us to see this phenomenon of Married Roommates as bigger than us, as the silent epidemic it has become. Through you we gained the perspective that, while all couples are unique, when it comes to the important relationships in life, we are more alike than different.

Being more accepting and understanding of one another can help us to start taking back the extra care that has been lost in marriages, families, and friendships.

Let's do this together—as the community we are.

ABOUT THE AUTHORS

Talia and Allen Wagner met at Pepperdine University, where they were both pursuing advanced degrees in psychology. Not only were they neighbors in the sprawling metropolis of Los Angeles, but they shared a love for travel. A friendship was formed, which, over time, evolved into love, marriage, children, and a shared practice as marriage and family therapists in LA.

It was hardly smooth sailing. It didn't take long for them to realize that they didn't really know how to be married, that they were basically winging it, not always successfully. Through the years, it is a reality that has been mirrored back to them from many couples they've seen. No one taught them how to be married, to fight fairly, to avoid falling into a tit for tat, or to keep the romance alive when sometimes you can barely stand each other.

Seeing the great need in today's modern marriages for better tools to understand and work together, this marriage and family therapist duo have been guiding couples to success around the world for years. As part of their mission to educate as many couples as possible, they are hard at work to get their messages out to couples outside their reach who may desperately need it, in hopes of creating peace and happiness at home.

Allen Wagner was born and raised in New York but has made Los Angeles his home for the past twenty years. While he started in film development as a story editor, opportunities took him on a yearlong overseas adventure abroad. Upon returning to LA, he began Pepperdine University's Graduate School of Education and Psychology, where he and Talia met. While he no longer backpacks through Southeast Asia, Allen can often be found on the hiking trails around LA with his dog, watching the Clippers, searching for a "good" Italian deli, or planning his next dive trip.

Talia Wagner, a California native, started her career in business and technology, where she was employed by several Fortune 500 companies. She is also a writer and lifelong learner who has traveled extensively, backpacked in the Himalayas, and almost met the Dalai Lama. It was traveling that solidified her interest in relationships and nudged her toward psychology and Pepperdine University.

Together, the Wagners make their home in Los Angeles with their children and are in private practice as marriage and family therapists.

Made in the USA
Monee, IL
15 April 2022

94778574R00134